Social Studies

myWorld
INTERACTIVE

1

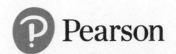
Pearson

Boston, Massachusetts   **Chandler, Arizona**
Glenview, Illinois   **New York, New York**

Pearson would like to extend a special thank you to all of the teachers who helped guide the development of this program. We gratefully acknowledge your efforts to realize the possibilities of elementary Social Studies teaching and learning. Together, we will prepare students for college, careers, and civic life.

Cover: Jim Cummins/Getty Images

Credits appear on pages R27–R28, which constitute an extension of this copyright page.

ISBN-13: 978-0-328-97308-8
ISBN-10: 0-328-97308-4

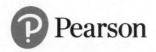

Program Authors

Dr. Linda B. Bennett
Faculty, Social Studies Education
College of Education
University of Missouri
Columbia, MO

Dr. James B. Kracht
Professor Emeritus
Departments of Geography and
    Teaching, Learning, and Culture
Texas A&M University
College Station, TX

Reviewers and Consultants

Program Consultants

ELL Consultant
Jim Cummins Ph.D.

Professor Emeritus,
Department of
    Curriculum, Teaching,
    and Learning
University of Toronto
Toronto, Canada

Differentiated Instruction Consultant

Kathy Tuchman Glass
President of Glass
    Educational Consulting
Woodside, CA

Reading Consultant
Elfrieda H. Hiebert Ph.D.

Founder, President and
    CEO, TextProject, Inc.
University of California
    Santa Cruz

Inquiry and C3 Consultant

Dr. Kathy Swan
Professor of Curriculum
    and Instruction
University of Kentucky
Lexington, KY

Academic Reviewers

Paul Apodaca, Ph.D.

Associate Professor,
    American Studies
Chapman University
Orange, CA

Warren J. Blumenfeld, Ed.D.

Former Associate
    Professor, Iowa State
    University, School
    of Education
South Hadley, MA

Dr. Albert M. Camarillo

Professor of History,
    Emeritus
Stanford University
Palo Alto, CA

Dr. Shirley A. James Hanshaw

Professor, Department
    of English
Mississippi State
    University
Mississippi State, MS

Xiaojian Zhao

Professor, Department
    of Asian American
    Studies
University of California,
    Santa Barbara
Santa Barbara, CA

Teacher Reviewers

Mercedes Kirk
First grade teacher
Folsom Cordova USD
Folsom, CA

Julie Martire
Teacher, Grade 5
Flocktown Elementary School
Long Valley, NJ

Kristy H. Spears
K-5 Reading Specialist
Pleasant Knoll Elementary School
Fort Mill, SC

Kristin Sullens
Teacher, Grade 4
Chula Vista ESD
San Diego, CA

Program Partner

Campaign for the Civic Mission of Schools is a coalition of over 70 national civic learning, education, civic engagement, and business groups committed to improving the quality and quantity of civic learning in American schools.

CAMPAIGN FOR THE CIVIC MISSION OF SCHOOLS

Educating for Democracy

⊕ Map and Graph Skills Handbook

✎ Writing Workshop

▤Q Using Primary and Secondary Sources

Chapter 1
Rights and Responsibilities of Citizens

GO ONLINE FOR
DIGITAL RESOURCES

📖 eTEXT

▶️ VIDEO

Big Question Video
Who is responsible for
making and enforcing
rules?

🔊 AUDIO

Sing About It! lyrics
and music

👆 INTERACTIVITY

• **Big Question
  Activity**
  Who is responsible
  for making and
  enforcing rules?
• **Quest Interactivities**
  Quest Kick Off,
  Quest Connections,
  Quest Findings
• **Lesson Interactivities**
  Lesson Introduction,
  Lesson Review
• **Digital Skill Practice**
  Distinguish Fact
  From Fiction,
  Solve a Problem

🎮 GAMES

Vocabulary Practice

☑️ ASSESSMENT

Lesson Quizzes and
Chapter Tests

The **BIG** Question Who is responsible for making and enforcing rules?

Geography of the Community

GO ONLINE FOR DIGITAL RESOURCES

 eTEXT

VIDEO

Big Question Video
What is the world like?

 AUDIO

Sing About It! lyrics and music

 INTERACTIVITY

- **Big Question Activity**
  What is the world like?

- **Quest Interactivities**
  Quest Kick Off,
  Quest Connections,
  Quest Findings

- **Lesson Interactivities**
  Lesson Introduction,
  Lesson Review

- **Digital Skill Practice**
  Ask and Answer
  Questions,
  Summarize

 GAMES

Vocabulary Practice

 ASSESSMENT

Lesson Quizzes and
Chapter Tests

The BIG Question   What is the world like?

Chapter 3

Symbols and Traditions of the United States

GO ONLINE FOR DIGITAL RESOURCES

 eTEXT

▶ VIDEO

Big Question Video
What does it mean to be American?

🔊 AUDIO

Sing About It! lyrics and music

👆 INTERACTIVITY

- **Big Question Activity**
  What does it mean to be American?
- **Quest Interactivities**
  Quest Kick Off,
  Quest Connections,
  Quest Findings
- **Lesson Interactivities**
  Lesson Introduction,
  Lesson Review
- **Digital Skill Practice**
  Cause and Effect,
  Analyze Images

 GAMES

Vocabulary Practice

☑ ASSESSMENT

Lesson Quizzes and Chapter Tests

The BIG Question What does it mean to be American?

Chapter 4 Life Today and Long Ago

GO ONLINE FOR DIGITAL RESOURCES

eTEXT

VIDEO

Big Question Video
How does life change throughout history?

AUDIO

Sing About It! lyrics and music

INTERACTIVITY

- **Big Question Activity**
  How does life change throughout history?
- **Quest Interactivities**
  Quest Kick Off,
  Quest Connections,
  Quest Findings
- **Lesson Interactivities**
  Lesson Introduction,
  Lesson Review
- **Digital Skill Practice**
  Interpret Timelines,
  Compare and Contrast

GAMES

Vocabulary Practice

ASSESSMENT

Lesson Quizzes and Chapter Tests

The BIG Question: How does life change throughout history?

Chapter 5

One Nation, Many People

GO ONLINE FOR DIGITAL RESOURCES

📖 eTEXT

▶ VIDEO

Big Question Video
How do so many different people make one nation?

🔊 AUDIO

Sing About It! lyrics and music

👆 INTERACTIVITY

• **Big Question Activity**
How do so many different people make one nation?

• **Quest Interactivities**
Quest Kick Off,
Quest Connections,
Quest Findings

• **Lesson Interactivities**
Lesson Introduction,
Lesson Review

• **Digital Skill Practice**
Compare Points of View, Sequence

🎮 GAMES

Vocabulary Practice

☑ ASSESSMENT

Lesson Quizzes and Chapter Tests

The BIG Question How do so many different people make one nation?

Chapter 6 Work in the Community

GO ONLINE FOR DIGITAL RESOURCES

 eTEXT

 VIDEO

Big Question Video
How do people get what they need?

 AUDIO

Sing About It! lyrics and music

INTERACTIVITY

- **Big Question Activity**
  How do people get what they need?
- **Quest Interactivities**
  Quest Kick Off,
  Quest Connections,
  Quest Findings
- **Lesson Interactivities**
  Lesson Introduction,
  Lesson Review
- **Digital Skill Practice**
  Identify Main
  Idea and Details,
  Analyze Costs and
  Benefits

 GAMES

Vocabulary Practice

ASSESSMENT

Lesson Quizzes and
Chapter Tests

The BIG Question   How do people get what they need?

Quests

Ask questions, explore sources, and cite evidence to support your view!

Maps

Where did this happen? Find out on these maps in your text.

Maps continued

Graphs and Charts

Find these charts, graphs, and tables in your text. They'll help you pull it together.

Silt 15%
Sand 25%
Water 60%

Primary Sources

Read primary sources to hear voices from the time.

People to Know

Read about the people who made history.

Citizenship

Biographies Online

Bella Abzug

Abigail Adams

Jane Addams

Susan B. Anthony

Clara Barton

Chaz Bono

Daniel Boone

Ruby Bridges

Juan Rodriguez Cabrillo

George Washington Carver

César Chávez

Sophie Cubbison

Marie Sklodowska Curie

Charles Drew

Henri Dunant

Thomas Edison

Albert Einstein

Benjamin Franklin

Betty Friedan

Dolores Huerta

Billie Jean King

Martin Luther King, Jr.

Yuri Kochiyama

Abraham Lincoln

Iqbal Masih

Golda Meir

Harvey Milk

José Montoya

John Muir

Gavin Newsom

Florence Nightingale

Rosa Parks

Louis Pasteur

Pocahontas

Sally Ride

Jackie Robinson

Eleanor Roosevelt

Wilma Rudolph

Jonas Salk

José Julio Sarria

George Shima

Sitting Bull

Gloria Steinem

Harriet Tubman

Booker T. Washington

George Washington

Malala Yousafzai

Skills

Practice key skills in these skills lessons.

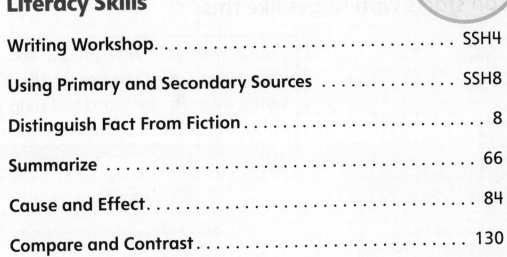

Literacy Skills

Critical Thinking Skills

Map and Graph Skills

Welcome to Your Book!

Your worktext is made up of chapters and lessons. Each lesson starts with pages like this.

> **Look for these words as you read.**

> **Words with yellow highlight are important social studies words. The sentence with the word will help you understand what the word means.**

Lesson
6 Making Choices in Government

Unlock The BIG Question

I will know how we choose our leaders.

🔵 INTERACTIVITY

Participate in a class discussion to preview the content of this lesson.

Vocabulary
vote
democracy
ballot

Academic Vocabulary
debate

JUMpstart Activity
Act out how you choose between two or more things.

How We Choose Our Leaders

Citizens vote to decide who they want to have as a leader. To **vote** is to make a choice that gets counted. Each person votes one time when they choose a leader. Citizens think about who will make the best leader.

1. ☑ **Reading Check** Main Idea and Details **Circle** a reason that citizens vote.

Direct Democracy

We can vote and make our own classroom decisions in a direct **democracy**. We can decide what game to play on a rainy day. One way we vote is to raise our hands. Then our teacher counts the votes. Another way is to use a **ballot**. A ballot is a sheet of paper used to make a secret vote. Every person takes part in making a decision when we vote.

2. ☑ **Reading Check** **Underline** the ways we vote.

> **Reading Checks will help you make sure you understood what you read.**

Your Turn!

Flip through your book with a partner.

1. Find the start of another lesson. What do you see on the page?

This book will give you a lot of chances to figure things out. Then you can show what you have figured out and give your reasons.

The Quest Kick Off will tell you the goal of the Quest.

You can get started right away.

Watch for Quest Connections all through the chapter.

Chapter 1

Quest
Project-Based Learning

Storyteller Sam Needs a Skit

Quest Kick Off

Most of you know the story of Cinderella and all the chores she had to do. Her stepsisters never helped. Luckily they have changed their ways. Can you help me write a skit to show everyone how to be fair?

1. **Start With a Brainstorm**
Think about the chores Cinderella does. *Why isn't it fair for one person to do all the work? What would be fair?* Write down ideas about how to share the chores.

INTERACTIVITY
Explore different ways people can be fair.

2. **Look for** *Quest* **Connections**
Turn to the next page to begin looking for your Quest Connections.

3. **Write Up Your** *Quest* **Findings**
At the end of the chapter, use what you learned to write and act out a skit.

2

The end of the chapter has Quest Findings. You will write or have a discussion or make something. Share what you figured out with other people.

2. Find two words with yellow highlight. What are they?

3. Find another Reading Check. What does it ask you to do?

4. Find another Quest. What is it called?

Learn to use important skills.

> Read the explanation. Look at all the text and pictures.

> Practice the skill. You'll be ready to use it whenever you need it.

Critical Thinking Skills

Analyze Costs and Benefits

When you spend money, you must make choices. Every choice has a cost. The cost is what you give up when you make a choice. The benefit is what you get in return.

You may have to choose between two toys. The benefit is the toy you chose. One cost is the money you paid for that toy. Another cost is the toy that you did not choose. When you chose not to buy that toy, you gave it up.

Your Turn!

Jen has saved enough money to buy a basketball or a game. **Look** at the chart.

INTERACTIVITY
Review and practice what you learned about costs and benefits.

1. What would you choose? **Mark** an X in a box to show your choice.

Jen's Choices				
Activity	Benefits	Cost (What you pay)	Cost (What you give up)	Choice
Game	1. Play inside or outside 2. Play with others	$15	the basketball	☐
Basketball	1. Play outside 2. Play with others or alone	$20		☐

2. What does Jen give up if she chooses the basketball? **Write** the answer on the line in the chart.

Your Turn!

Work with a partner.

1. Find another skill lesson. What skill will you learn? Talk about another time you might need that skill.

Every chapter has primary source pages.
You can read or look at these sources to
learn right from people who were there.

Find out what this source is
about and who made it.

These questions help you
think about the source.

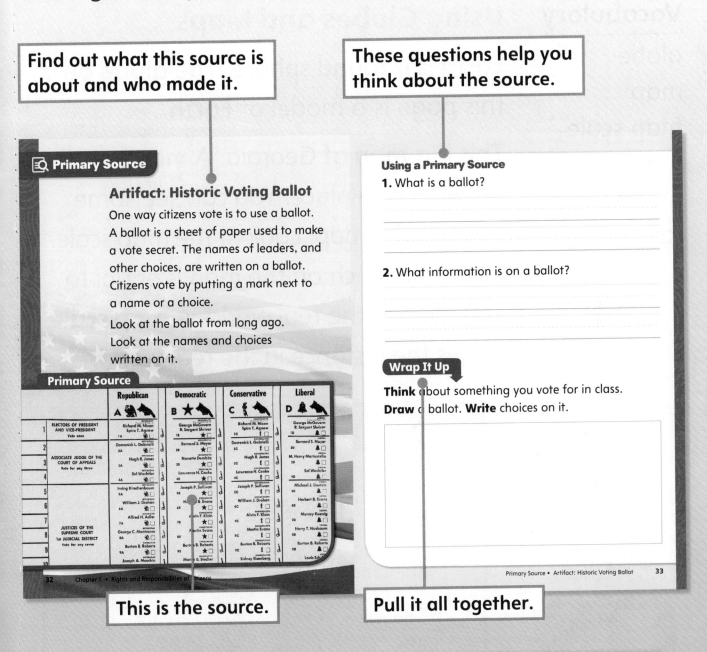

Primary Source

Artifact: Historic Voting Ballot

One way citizens vote is to use a ballot.
A ballot is a sheet of paper used to make
a vote secret. The names of leaders, and
other choices, are written on a ballot.
Citizens vote by putting a mark next to
a name or a choice.

Look at the ballot from long ago.
Look at the names and choices
written on it.

Primary Source

32   Chapter 1 • Rights and Responsibilities of Citizens

Using a Primary Source

1. What is a ballot?

2. What information is on a ballot?

Wrap It Up

Think about something you vote for in class.
Draw a ballot. **Write** choices on it.

Primary Source • Artifact: Historic Voting Ballot   33

This is the source.

Pull it all together.

2. Find another primary source lesson in your book.
   What is the source about?

Map and Graph Skills Handbook

Vocabulary

globe
map
map scale
map legend
graph
tally

Using Globes and Maps

Earth is a round sphere. The **globe** on this page is a model of Earth.

This is a **map** of Georgia. A map is a drawing of a place. You can see some cities on the map. Look at the map scale. Nearly one inch on the map is equal to 100 miles in the real world. A **map scale** shows the distance in the real world.

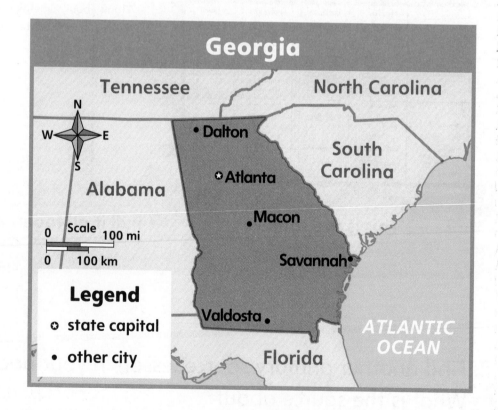

Georgia

Tennessee

North Carolina

N
W E
S

• Dalton

South Carolina

Alabama

✪ Atlanta

• Macon

Scale
0   100 mi
0   100 km

Savannah •

Legend
✪ state capital
• other city

Valdosta •

ATLANTIC OCEAN

Florida

This map shows a community. The **map legend**, or map key, shows what the symbols mean. You can see that the school is next to the park.

1. ☑Reading Check **Circle** the map scale on the map of Georgia. **Draw** another type of building on the community map. **Put** a symbol for that building on the map legend.

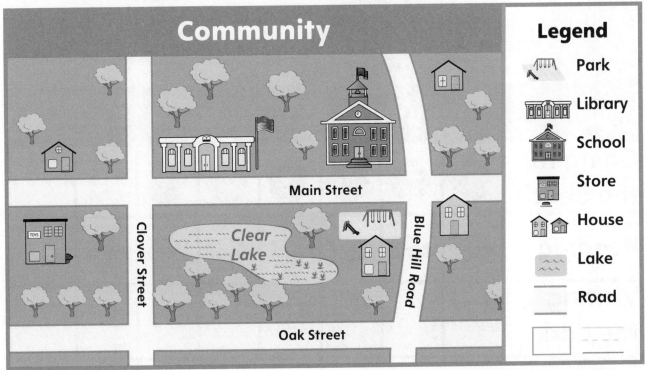

Picture Graphs

A **graph** is a diagram that shows information. Some children voted on their favorite activity. Each child put a picture on the graph. A picture shows each child's choice.

2. ☑ Reading Check **Look** at the picture graph. **Write** the name of the activity with the most votes.

_____

Favorite Activities

Going to the Beach	🏐	🏐	🏐	🏐	🏐	🏐		
Reading	📖	📖	📖	📖	📖	📖	📖	
Visiting the Park	🛝	🛝	🛝	🛝				

Other Graphs

A bar graph or a tally graph could also show the choices. Each colored box or **tally** mark shows one choice.

3. ✅Reading Check **Look** at the bar graph. **Complete** the missing row to show seven votes for reading.

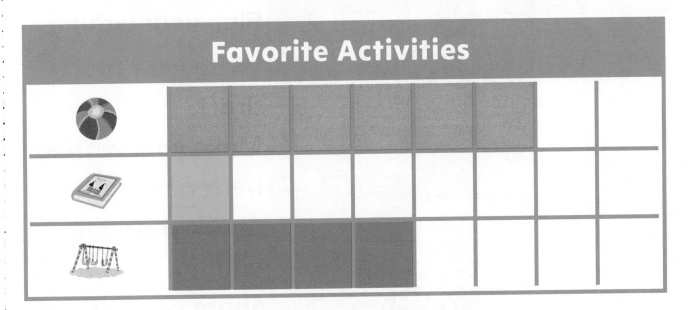

Writing Workshop

Keys to Good Writing

Good writers follow steps when they write. Here are five steps that will help you become a good writer!

Prewrite	Plan your writing.
Draft	Write your first draft.
Revise	Make your writing better.
Edit	Check your writing.
Share	Share your writing with others.

Writing Genres

Opinion

Write what you think about a topic. Give reasons for your opinion. Add details.

Information

Explain a topic. Write ideas and facts. Use images to show details.

Narrative

Write a story. Tell events in the order they happened. Give details about the events.

1. ☑ **Reading Check** Which games do children play at recess? **Give** facts and details about a game. **Give** reasons for your opinion.

_____

_____

_____

_____

Using the Library Media Center

How do you do research? Start in the Library Media Center. There are materials on many topics. Ask the librarian to help you.

2. ☑ Reading Check Work with a partner to research a topic. **Ask and answer** two questions.

Using the Internet

You can do research on the Internet. Use key words to search. Ask the librarian about each site you find.

Be Safe on the Internet

Ask an adult for help. Never give anyone on the Internet:

- your full name
- your address
- your phone number

3. ☑ Reading Check **Write** a narrative about a child who uses the Internet safely. Use a separate sheet of paper.

Using Primary and Secondary Sources

Vocabulary

document
artifact
primary
 source
secondary
 source
biography

Using Primary and Secondary Sources

Sources can tell us about life in the past. You can read a **document**, or a paper with words. You can look at an **artifact**, or an object made by people. Study each source closely to see if it can answer your questions.

Primary Sources

A **primary source** is made by a person who was at an event. This very old pottery is a primary source.

1. ☑ Reading Check How can this source tell you about life long ago? **Turn** and **tell** a friend.

Secondary Sources

A **secondary source** is made after an event happened. The person who creates the source was not at the event. If you write about an artifact, you create a secondary source.

Primary and secondary sources tell us who, where, when, and how. Asking questions about the sources helps us learn.

This secondary source tells about early explorers.

2. ✅ **Reading Check** How is a primary source different from a secondary source? **Write** one sentence to explain.

_____

_____

_____

_____

Examples of Primary and Secondary Sources

When you write in a journal, you create a primary source. Photographs, maps, and paintings can be primary sources.

Your textbook is a secondary source. Many library books are secondary sources. A **biography** is a book about someone's life. It is written by another person.

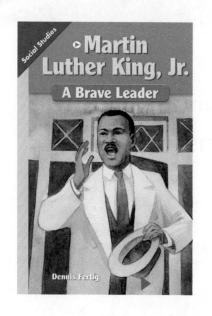

3. ☑ **Reading Check** **Ask** a question about the painting. **Underline** examples of secondary sources.

_____

_____

_____

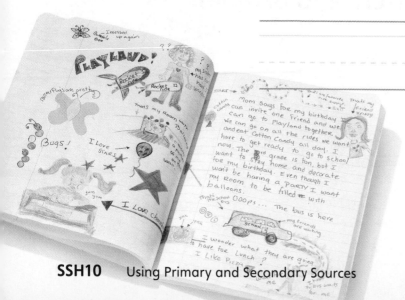

Primary and Secondary Sources

Study the sources below. Some are primary sources. Some are secondary sources.

4. ☑ **Reading Check** **Circle** the secondary sources. **Write** how you can tell the photograph is a primary source.

_____

_____

_____

_____

an encyclopedia

a photograph

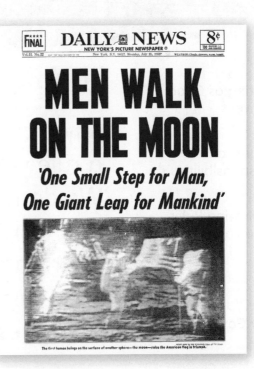

a newspaper article

a history project

Chapter 1
Rights and Responsibilities of Citizens

GO ONLINE FOR
DIGITAL RESOURCES

- ▶ VIDEO
- 👆 INTERACTIVITY
- 🔊 AUDIO
- 🎮 GAMES
- ☑ ASSESSMENT
- 📖 eTEXT

The BIG Question

▶ VIDEO

Who is responsible for making and enforcing rules?

Jumpstart Activity

👆 INTERACTIVITY

Say a clue to a partner about a rule you follow. For example: We do this when we want to talk (raise our hands). Have your partner guess the rule. Take turns giving clues and guessing.

We Have Rights

Preview the chapter **vocabulary** by singing the song to the tune of "The Farmer in the Dell."

Government leaders make the laws
In our democracy.

Citizen's rights are earned
Through responsibility.

The mayor leads the city.

The governor leads the state.

The president leads our country.

Oh, the system's pretty great!

1

Quest
Project-Based Learning

Storyteller Sam Needs a Skit

Quest Kick Off

Most of you know the story of Cinderella and all the chores she had to do. Her stepsisters never helped. Luckily they have changed their ways. Can you help me write a skit to show everyone how to be fair?

1 Start With a Brainstorm

Think about the chores Cinderella does. *Why isn't it fair for one person to do all the work? What would be fair?* Write down ideas about how to share the chores.

 INTERACTIVITY

Explore different ways people can be fair.

2 Look for Quest Connections

Turn to the next page to begin looking for your Quest Connections.

3 Write Up Your Quest Findings

At the end of the chapter, use what you learned to write and act out a skit.

Acting as Good Citizens

I will know how to be a good citizen.

Participate in a class discussion to preview the content of this lesson.

Vocabulary

citizen
rule

JumpStart Activity

Take turns telling a partner the nice things you do for others.

Help, Respect, and Listen

A **citizen** is a person who belongs to a state or country. Good citizens help and respect each other. They listen to others and work to make life better for all.

1. ☑ **Reading Check** Main Idea and Details **Underline** what good citizens do.

Rules We Follow

Good citizens follow rules. A **rule** tells us what to do and what not to do. Rules help us learn. For example, we take turns when we talk about something important. We share books and crayons. Everyone helps to clean up after working.

We follow the Golden Rule. We treat each other the way we want to be treated. Then others are nice to us!

2. ☑ **Reading Check** **Cause and Effect** **Circle** what can happen when we follow the Golden Rule.

 **Quest Connection**

Underline an example of making a game fair for everyone.

INTERACTIVITY

Learn more about playing fair.

Being a Good Sport

It can feel good when your team wins a game, but you do not win every time you play. Sometimes your team loses. How you act during and after a game shows if you are a good sport.

Ways to Be a Good Sport

Play fair and follow game rules.
Give everyone a chance to play.
Shake hands with members of the other team.
Say "Nice try!" or "Great job!"

3. ☑ **Reading Check** **Write** a way that you will be a good sport. **Talk** to a partner about it.

_____

_____

_____

_____

4. Sequence Write something that is important to do after playing a game.

_____

_____

_____

5. Draw a picture. **Show** a rule you follow that helps you to learn or work.

6. Understand the _Quest_ **Connection Talk** with a partner. **Tell** about a time you played fair.

Distinguish Fact From Fiction

Some sentences give facts. A fact is true.
Some sentences are fiction. Fiction is
not true. It is something that is
made up.

Look at the pictures and read the
sentences. Think about how one is true
and one is not true.

Fact:

Fiction:

Abraham Lincoln was a
leader who lived long ago.
He treated people with
respect and kindness.

Crocodile did not follow
the Golden Rule.
He tricked Monkey.

Your Turn!

1. Look at the pictures.

Read the sentences.

Circle the sentence that gives a fact.

Highlight the sentence that is fiction.

 INTERACTIVITY

Review and practice what you learned about how to tell fact from fiction.

Little Red Riding Hood brought a basket of food to her sick grandmother.

Susan B. Anthony was a leader who wanted women to be treated as equals.

2. Draw a picture that is fact and one that is fiction.

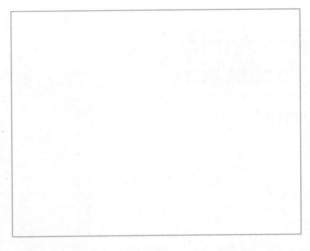

Unlock The BIG Question

I will know about my rights and responsibilities.

👆 INTERACTIVITY

Participate in a class discussion to preview the content of this lesson.

Vocabulary

right
responsibility
cooperate

Academic Vocabulary

solve

JumpStart Activity

Ask two other children what they think *responsibility* means.

We Have Rights

All citizens have rights. A **right** is something we are free to do or have. Going to school is a right. Speaking up is a right and so is joining a group. Being treated fairly when we play is a right, too.

1. ☑ **Reading Check** **Main Idea and Details** **Underline** the main idea. **Circle** detail sentences.

We Have Responsibilities

We have responsibilities at home and school. A **responsibility** is something we do because we have to or because it is the right thing. We may clean our room and set the table as our home jobs. We may feed the fish and hand out paper as our class jobs.

2. ☑Reading Check **Write** a responsibility you have at home or school.

_____

_____

_____

We Cooperate

Quest Connection

Tell how you share responsibilities at school.

INTERACTIVITY

Explore ways to make responsibilities fair.

Another responsibility we have is to cooperate. We **cooperate** when we work together. We show respect and do not bully our classmates.

We Solve Problems

Sometimes we have problems when we work in groups. For example, when we only have one of something to share. We talk to each other to **solve** the problem.

Academic Vocabulary

solve • to fix a problem

3. ☑ Reading Check **Talk** to a partner. **Tell** how you cooperate.

☑ Lesson 2 Check

4. Summarize Write what you would do if your group only had one of something to share.

_____

_____

_____

_____

5. Draw a picture. **Show** a right that you have.

6. Understand the *Quest* Connection **Finish** the sentence.
At school, we share responsibilities by

_____

_____

_____

_____

Lesson 2 • Rights and Responsibilities   **13**

Lesson 3 Following Rules and Laws

Unlock The BIG Question

I will know about rules and laws that we follow.

INTERACTIVITY

Participate in a class discussion to preview the content of this lesson.

Vocabulary

law
consequence

Academic Vocabulary

cause

JumpStart Activity

Act out a rule you follow at home, at school, or in your community.

Rules at Home

Rules are made to keep us healthy and safe. We brush our teeth. We wash our hands before eating. We pick up toys so no one trips and gets hurt. We do not run up and down stairs.

1. ☑ **Reading Check** Main Idea and Details **Circle** the main idea about safety rules. **Highlight** the details.

Rules at School

Rules help us get along. It is important to respect and be nice to others. We take turns and share. We keep our hands to ourselves. We are good sports.

Rules keep things fair, too. Everyone must follow the rules in order for them to work well.

2. ☑ **Reading Check** **Underline a rule that helps you get along with others.**

Rules and Laws in the Community

Quest Connection

What are some rules that you are responsible for following?

INTERACTIVITY

Learn about ways to follow rules and be fair.

A community rule is called a **law**. It is a law that children must go to school so they can learn. Putting trash where it belongs is a law that keeps our community clean. Wearing a seat belt in a car keeps us safe. Wearing a helmet when we ride a bike keeps us safe, too.

3. ☑Reading Check **Look** at the picture. **Circle** the part that shows a safety law.

Consequences

A **consequence** is what happens when we do not follow rules and laws. Drivers can **cause** accidents if they do not stop at a red light. We can get hurt if we do not wear a seat belt. Good citizens follow rules and laws.

Academic Vocabulary

cause •
the reason something happens

INTERACTIVITY

Check your understanding of the key ideas of this lesson.

☑ Lesson 3 Check

4. Cause and Effect If you do not follow the rules, what is a consequence in class?

_____

_____

_____

5. Write why rules are important to follow.

_____

_____

_____

6. Understand the *Quest* Connection **Talk** to a partner about a school rule that helps you get along with others.

Solve a Problem

A problem is something to be worked out.

A solution is a way to solve the problem. Here is a child that is being bullied.

1. Identify the problem.

2. Gather information about it.

3. List ways to solve it.

4. Ask: "Which way will work best?"

5. Choose a way and solve the problem.

6. Think about how well your plan worked.

1. What is the problem? **Use** the steps you learned to solve the problem.

INTERACTIVITY

Review and practice what you learned about solving a problem.

I want to keep using the computer.

I want to use the computer now.

2. Draw a picture. **Show** one way to solve the problem. **Tell** why this plan works best.

Lesson 4 My Leaders

Unlock The BIG Question

I will know who leaders are and how they help us.

INTERACTIVITY

Participate in a class discussion to preview the content of this lesson.

Vocabulary

leader
guardian

Academic Vocabulary

create

JumpStart Activity

Tell about someone who makes rules. Draw a picture of this person.

Who Are Leaders?

A **leader** helps people decide what to do and how to do it. Leaders make rules. They make sure we follow rules, too. There are leaders who help us at home and at school. Some leaders help us in the community.

1. ☑ **Reading Check** Main Idea and Details **Underline** what leaders do.

Leaders at Home

A **guardian** is a leader who takes care of us at home. Our mothers, fathers, and grandparents are guardians and leaders. An older brother or sister can be a leader, too. They make sure we follow the rules. The rules they make are for our health and safety. These rules can also help everyone get along.

2. ☑ **Reading Check** **Highlight leaders who help you at home.**

Word Wise

Suffixes
The word *leader* ends in *-er*. This ending means "someone who." *Leader* means "someone who leads." What does *teacher* mean?

Academic Vocabulary

create •
to make something

Teachers, principals, and coaches **create** rules when they are needed. Rules help us learn and be safe. They help us work and play together.

Sometimes it is our turn to be school leaders. We can be a table leader or a captain of a team.

3. ☑ **Reading Check** **Look** at the picture. **Write** what the child is doing.

_____

_____

_____

Leaders in the Community

There are leaders in the community who keep us safe. Firefighters keep us safe from fires. Police officers make sure people follow traffic laws.

INTERACTIVITY

Check your understanding of the key ideas of this lesson.

☑ Lesson 4 Check

4. How are leaders at home, school, and the community similar?

_____

_____

5. Draw a school leader. **Show** how this person helps you.

6. Tell who makes sure you follow school rules.

5 My Government

I will know how government helps us.

🖐 **INTERACTIVITY**

Participate in a class discussion to preview the content of this lesson.

Vocabulary

government
mayor
governor
president

JumpStart Activity

Talk to a partner. What would happen if we did not follow rules or laws?

What Is a Government?

A **government** is made up of citizens. These citizens make our laws and make sure we follow them. They get us what we need. They make sure where we live is clean and safe.

1. ☑️ **Reading Check** **Look** at the picture. **Circle** what is safe in this community. **Talk** about it.

Community Government

A **mayor** is the leader of a community government. The mayor works with other leaders to make community laws. These leaders determine if we need a stop sign. They make sure trash is picked up. They decide if we need to plant trees or flowers in a park. They make sure there are police officers to keep us safe.

2. ☑ Reading Check Main Idea and Details **Highlight** the work that community government does.

State Capitol building in Springfield, Illinois

State Government

A **governor** is the leader of a state. The governor works with other leaders to make state laws. They spend money to build or fix highways, tunnels, and bridges. They make sure we have schools and state parks. Then children can enjoy learning and playing in these places!

State leaders meet in the capital city. This is where they make important decisions.

3. ☑ Reading Check **Circle what the state government spends its money on.**

National Government

The **president** is the leader of our country. The president works with the leaders of Congress to make our country's laws. These laws keep us safe and make sure we are treated fairly.

INTERACTIVITY

Check your understanding of the key ideas of this lesson.

☑ Lesson 5 Check

4. Compare and Contrast What is similar about community, state, and national government?

_____

_____

_____

_____

5. Finish the sentence.
Government builds schools and _____ so children can learn and play.

6. Tell how a mayor and governor are alike.

_____

_____

_____

_____

_____

Lesson 6 Making Choices in Government

Unlock The BIG Question

I will know how we choose our leaders.

INTERACTIVITY

Participate in a class discussion to preview the content of this lesson.

Vocabulary

vote
democracy
ballot

Academic Vocabulary

debate

Jumpstart Activity

Act out how you choose between two or more things.

How We Choose Our Leaders

Citizens vote to decide who they want to have as a leader. To **vote** is to make a choice that gets counted. Each person votes one time when they choose a leader. Citizens think about who will make the best leader.

1. ☑ **Reading Check** Main Idea and Details **Circle** a reason that citizens vote.

VOTE

Direct Democracy

We can vote and make our own classroom decisions in a direct **democracy**. We can decide what game to play on a rainy day. One way we vote is to raise our hands. Then our teacher counts the votes. Another way is to use a **ballot**. A ballot is a sheet of paper used to make a secret vote. Every person takes part in making a decision when we vote.

2. ☑ **Reading Check** **Underline** the **ways we vote.**

Representative Democracy

Sometimes we choose classroom leaders or table leaders. This is called a representative democracy. These leaders will make decisions for us. They help us decide what to do or how we do it. We listen to different leaders **debate** before we vote for them. It is important to understand what leaders believe. We want to make sure the leader we choose will work hard for us.

Academic Vocabulary

debate • to talk about something

3. ☑ Reading Check **Highlight who makes decisions in a classroom representative democracy.**

The Differences

Every citizen votes in a direct democracy. It is our responsibility to learn about the issues before we vote.

In a representative democracy, citizens vote for leaders to make decisions for us.

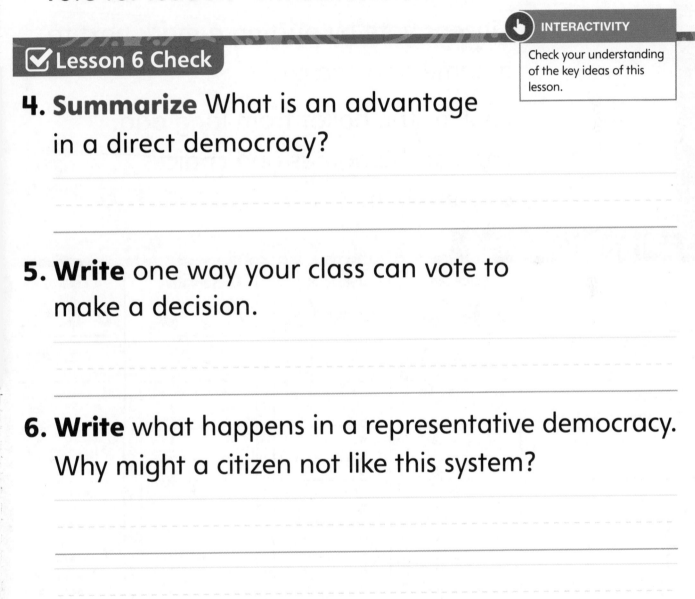

INTERACTIVITY

Check your understanding of the key ideas of this lesson.

☑ Lesson 6 Check

4. **Summarize** What is an advantage in a direct democracy?

_____

_____

_____

5. **Write** one way your class can vote to make a decision.

_____

_____

_____

6. **Write** what happens in a representative democracy. Why might a citizen not like this system?

_____

_____

_____

_____

Artifact: Historic Voting Ballot

One way citizens vote is to use a ballot. A ballot is a sheet of paper used to make a vote secret. The names of leaders, and other choices, are written on a ballot. Citizens vote by putting a mark next to a name or a choice.

Look at the ballot from long ago. Look at the names and choices written on it.

Primary Source

		Republican	Democratic	Conservative	Liberal
		A	**B**	**C**	**D**
1	ELECTORS OF PRESIDENT AND VICE-PRESIDENT Vote once	REPUBLICAN Presidential Electors for Richard M. Nixon Spiro T. Agnew 1A	DEMOCRATIC Presidential Electors for George McGovern R. Sargent Shriver 1B	CONSERVATIVE Presidential Electors for Richard M. Nixon Spiro T. Agnew 1C	LIBERAL Presidential Electors for George McGovern R. Sargent Shriver 1D
2		REPUBLICAN Domenick L. Gabrielli 2A	DEMOCRATIC Bernard S. Meyer 2B	CONSERVATIVE Domenick L. Gabrielli 2C	LIBERAL Bernard S. Meyer 2D
3	ASSOCIATE JUDGE OF THE COURT OF APPEALS Vote for any three	REPUBLICAN Hugh R. Jones 3A	DEMOCRATIC Nanette Dembitz 3B	CONSERVATIVE Hugh R. Jones 3C	LIBERAL M. Henry Martuscello 3D
4		REPUBLICAN Sol Wachtler 4A	DEMOCRATIC Lawrence H. Cooke 4B	CONSERVATIVE Lawrence H. Cooke 4C	LIBERAL Sol Wachtler 4D
5		REPUBLICAN Irving Kirschenbaum 5A	DEMOCRATIC Joseph P. Sullivan 5B	CONSERVATIVE Joseph P. Sullivan 5C	LIBERAL Michael J. Dontzin 5D
6		REPUBLICAN William J. Drohan 6A	DEMOCRATIC Herbert B. Evans 6B	CONSERVATIVE William J. Drohan 6C	LIBERAL Herbert B. Evans 6D
7		REPUBLICAN Alfred H. Adler 7A	DEMOCRATIC Alvin F. Klein 7B	CONSERVATIVE Alvin F. Klein 7C	LIBERAL Murray Koenig 7D
8	JUSTICES OF THE SUPREME COURT 1st JUDICIAL DISTRICT Vote for any seven	REPUBLICAN George C. Mantzoros 8A	DEMOCRATIC Martin Evans 8B	CONSERVATIVE Martin Evans 8C	LIBERAL Harry T. Nusbaum 8D
9		REPUBLICAN Burton B. Roberts 9A	DEMOCRATIC Burton B. Roberts 9B	CONSERVATIVE Burton B. Roberts 9C	LIBERAL Burton B. Roberts 9D
10		REPUBLICAN Joseph A. Macchia	DEMOCRATIC Martin B. Stecher	CONSERVATIVE Sidney Eisenberg	LIBERAL Louis Schi...

Using a Primary Source

1. What is a ballot?

_____

_____

_____

_____

2. What information is on a ballot?

_____

_____

_____

_____

Wrap It Up

Think about something you vote for in class.
Draw a ballot. **Write** choices on it.

★ Citizenship

Quality: Honesty

Abraham Lincoln
Honest Abe

Before Abraham Lincoln was our president, he was a store clerk and a lawyer. People knew him as "Honest Abe."

People told stories about Lincoln's honesty. One story is about when young Abe worked in a store. He walked many miles to return a few pennies to a customer. She had paid him too much money!

Tell how Abraham Lincoln was honest.

_____

_____

_____

_____

Talk About It

Turn and **talk** to a partner. **Tell** about how you are honest.

☑ Assessment

🎮 **GAMES**

Play the vocabulary game.

Vocabulary and Key Ideas

1. Fill in the circle next to the best answer. What is the Golden **Rule**?

Ⓐ Throw trash away in a trash can.

Ⓑ Line up quickly and quietly in class.

Ⓒ Treat others the way you want to be treated.

Ⓓ Raise your hand before speaking.

2. Distinguish Fact From Fiction Circle the sentence that is fiction. **Highlight** the fact.

Ant worked hard while Grasshopper played.

Good citizens help one another.

3. Draw a line. **Match** a leader to what each person leads.

president   community

mayor   state

governor   nation

4. Look at the picture.

Write a rule that would help to solve this problem.

_____

_____

_____

_____

Quest Findings

Write Your Skit

It's time to put it all together to write and act out your skit!

1 Plan and Write Your Skit

Work in a group. Who are the main characters? How do they show how to be fair?

2 Revise Your Skit

Make changes to your skit. Check that the skit shows how to be fair.

3 Cast Your Skit

Ask classmates to be in your skit. Then practice the lines and actions.

4 Perform Your Skit

Perform your skit for the class.

The BIG Question

What is the world like?

▶ VIDEO

JumpStart Activity

👆 INTERACTIVITY

Look at the photo. Tell what this community is like.

AUDIO

Show You Care

Preview the chapter **vocabulary** by singing the song to the tune of "Yankee Doodle."

You may live upon the **plains**
Or near a hill or lake.
Show you care about the earth.
There are simple steps to take!

Care for land and wildlife, too.
Let's take care of our nation.
Keep our air and water clean
And practice **conservation!**

Tina the Tour Leader Needs Your Help

Tina

Quest Kick Off

Hi! I'm Tina the tour leader. I need help writing about our state for my tours. I need to make a tour guide and a map that I can hand out to my tour groups. Then they can find fun and exciting places to visit!

tour starts here

1 Start with a Brainstorm

Think about what your state is like. What is the weather like? What are fun activities you can do on land and in the water? What are some interesting places to visit? Write down ideas about what the state is like.

INTERACTIVITY

Learn about how to make a tour.

_____

_____

_____

_____

_____

_____

_____

2 Look for Quest Connections

Turn to the next page to begin looking for your Quest Connections.

3 Write Up Your Quest Findings

At the end of the chapter, use what you know to make your tour guide and map. Then act out fun things people can do when they come to visit!

1 Our Community

I will know how to talk about relative location.

👆 **INTERACTIVITY**

Participate in a class discussion to preview the content of this lesson.

Vocabulary

community
city
town
location
relative
 location

Academic Vocabulary

describe

JumPstart Activity

Turn to a partner. Talk about places you like to visit near your home.

Where We Live

A **community** is a place where people and families live, work, and have fun. A **city** is a big community with many people. A **town** is a small community. It has fewer people than a city.

1. ✅ **Reading Check** Main Idea and Details **Underline** words that tell about two different kinds of communities.

What We Do

There are many things we can do in a community. Families go to the market to shop for food. Children go to school to learn. Sometimes we go see the doctor for a checkup. We go to the library where we can check out books to read at home. We can play at the park with friends.

2. ☑ **Reading Check** **Look** at the picture. **Circle** places that you visit in your community. **Tell** about each one.

above

next to

inside

Quest Connection

Role-play activities you can do in your community.

👆 **INTERACTIVITY**

Learn more about fun things to do in your community.

Academic Vocabulary

describe •
to tell about something

Places Near Us

Location tells where something is. **Relative location** tells where something is by comparing it to something else. You can use location words to **describe** where you are in your community.

Some location words are *near, next to, above, inside,* and *below.* Look at the pictures. The kite is above the girl. The boy is next to the bike. The family is inside the store.

3. ☑ **Reading Check** Use **Evidence From Text** **Circle** relative location words.

☑ Lesson 1 Check

4. Summary Describe what your community is like.

_____

_____

_____

_____

_____

5. Use location words to describe your school's relative location in the community.

_____

My school is _____

_____.

6. Understand the Quest Connection Draw a picture. **Show** an activity you do in your community.

Lesson 2 Finding Places

Unlock The BIG Question

I will know how to talk about absolute location.

INTERACTIVITY

Participate in a class discussion to preview the content of this lesson.

Vocabulary

absolute
location
map
direction
cardinal
directions

JumpStart Activity

Work in a small group. Take turns telling about where you live.

Compare Locations

You know that relative location tells where something is by comparing it to something else. **Absolute location** is the exact spot where a place is found.

1. ☑ **Reading Check** Compare and Contrast **Write** how relative and absolute location are similar.

_____

_____

_____

My Address

Your home address is an absolute location. It is the number of your home and the street where you live. It also includes your community's name and state. It is important to have an absolute location. A postal worker can deliver your family's mail. Your friends can come over when they know your address.

2. ☑ **Reading Check** **Write the absolute location of where you live.**

_____

_____

_____

_____

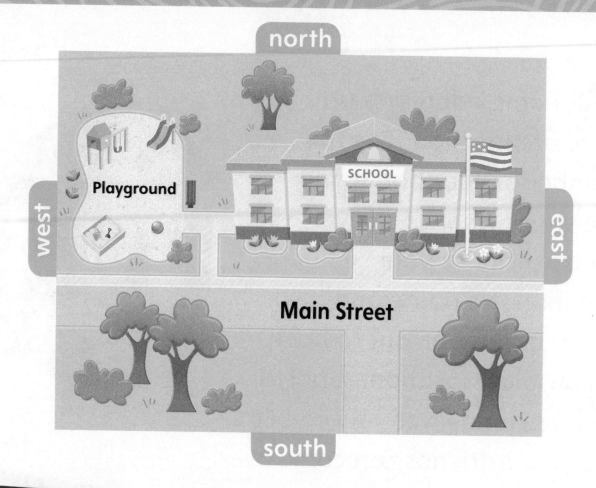

north

west

east

Playground

SCHOOL

Main Street

south

Word Wise

Multiple Meanings

What is another meaning for the word *direction*?

A Community Map

A **map** is a drawing of a place. It shows information about where things are located. A map shows what a place looks like from above. Maps can show you what direction to go to find a place, too. A **direction** tells which way to go or where something is.

3. ☑ **Reading Check** Draw Conclusions **Underline** how a map can be helpful.

Cardinal Directions

Maps show the **cardinal directions** *north*,
south, *east*, and *west*. Look at the map.
Put your finger on the playground.
Move your finger to the side marked *east*.
The school is east of the playground.

4. ☑**Reading Check** **Look** at the map.
   Tell what is west of the school.

INTERACTIVITY
Check your understanding
of the key ideas of this
lesson.

☑**Lesson 2 Check**

5. **Summarize Tell** why it is important
   to know the absolute location of your home.

6. **Work** with a partner. **Look** at a map of your state.
   Find your community or one near you on the map.
   Talk about its relative location to other places.

7. **Draw** a map on a separate piece of paper.
   Show your community. **Write** labels for your map.

Artifact: An Envelope

Today, we send messages to friends using e-mail. Long ago, there were no computers. People could only write letters to each other. They sent the letters in envelopes. They used postage stamps to pay for letters to be delivered.

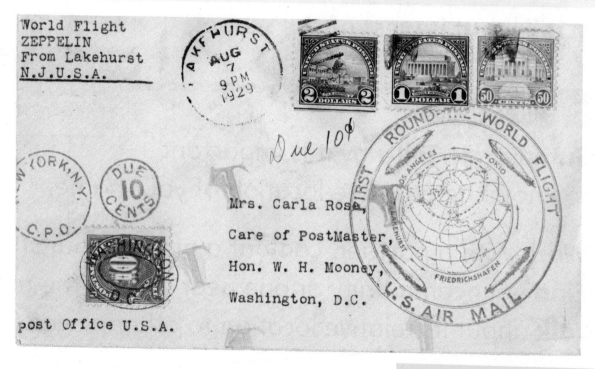

Look at this envelope. The letter is being sent to Mrs. Carla Rose. It was mailed from Lakehurst, New Jersey. The envelope has postage stamps, too.

Fun Fact

Long ago, it could take many weeks or months for a letter to be delivered.

Using a Primary Source

1. Where is this letter going?

_____

_____

2. Practice filling out an envelope. **Draw** an envelope. **Write** a friend's name and address in the center. **Write** your name and address in the top left corner. **Draw** a postage stamp in the top right corner.

[ ]

Wrap It Up

Write what you know about sending a letter.

_____

_____

_____

_____

Unlock The BIG Question

I will know about maps and models.

INTERACTIVITY

Participate in a class discussion to preview the content of this lesson.

Vocabulary

compass rose
symbol
legend

Academic Vocabulary

model

JumpStart Activity

Work with a partner. Take turns telling about maps you and your family have used. Tell why you needed to use them.

Parts of a Map

A map has different parts. A title tells the map's main idea. The points on a **compass rose** show cardinal directions. N stands for *north*, S for *south*, E for *east*, and W for *west*.

A map **symbol** is a picture that stands for a real thing.

The **legend**, or key, tells what the symbols on a map mean. Look at the map. The school symbol in the legend stands for the school on the map.

1. ☑**Reading Check** **Look** at the map. **Circle** the compass rose. **Underline** the symbol in the legend that stands for the library. **Write** the direction you would travel to get from the playground to the library.

_____

_____

_____

Quest Connection

What are words and symbols you would put in a legend?

INTERACTIVITY

Explore maps and symbols.

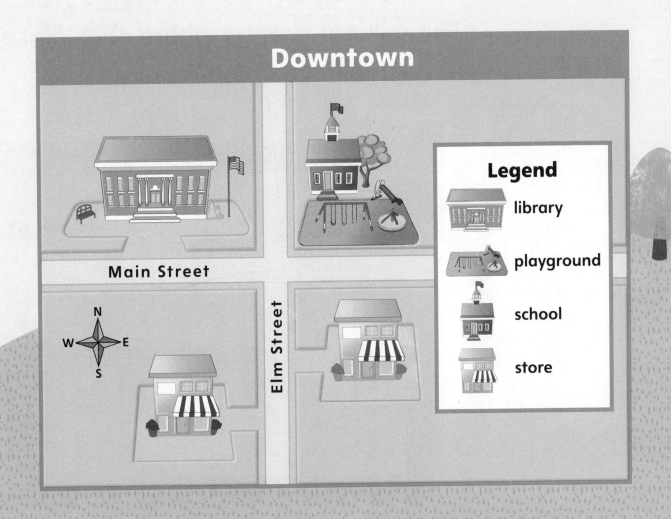

Downtown

Main Street

Elm Street

N
W   E
S

Legend

library

playground

school

store

Maps, Pictures, and Models

Academic Vocabulary

model • a 3-dimensional version of something, but much smaller

You can build a **model** of your community. It will look similar to your community. But the model will be a much smaller size, or scale. This is called a 3-D model. A model is not flat.

A map and a picture tell the same story as a model. They look like a model, but they are flat. You can hang a map or a picture on the wall. This will not change where each place is located in your community.

2. ☑**Reading Check** Compare and Contrast
Write how a model is similar to a map or a picture. **Write** how they are different.

Similar: _____

Different: _____

INTERACTIVITY

Check your understanding of the key ideas of this lesson.

☑**Lesson 3 Check**

3. With a partner, **draw** a map of your town. Use a separate piece of paper. Then use blocks to make a model.

4. Tell why a map has a compass rose.

5. Understand the *Quest* Connection **Draw** symbols you would put in the legend of your map.

Ask and Answer Questions

Ask yourself questions when you look at a map. Read the title to find out what it is. Look at the symbols in the legend. The symbols will help you understand how to read the map.

Look at the map of California. Ask yourself questions. Then answer each one. For example:

• What is the title of this map?

• What is the state capital of California?

• How do I know it is the state capital?

• Which two states are east of California?

1. **Look** at the map of California. **Circle** the title. **Underline** the name of the state capital. **Highlight** two states that are east of California.

2. **Take turns** with a partner. **Ask** and **answer** questions about information on the California map. **Use** the compass rose and the legend to help you.

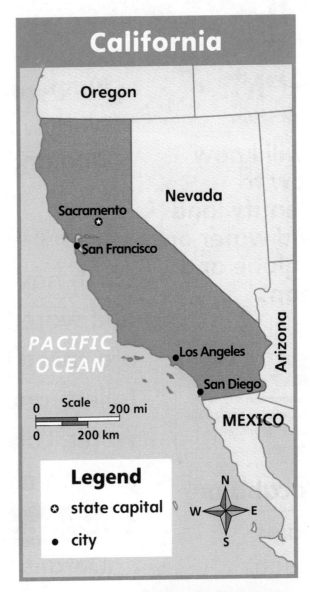

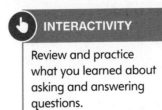

INTERACTIVITY

Review and practice what you learned about asking and answering questions.

Unlock The BIG Question

I will know how to identify land and water on a globe and map.

👆 INTERACTIVITY

Participate in a class discussion to preview the content of this lesson.

Vocabulary

plains
ocean
continent

JumpStart Activity

Work with a partner. Tell about the land and water where you live.

Land and Water

Earth has different kinds of land and water. Flat lands with few trees are called **plains**. Mountains are the tallest land. Rivers are long bodies of water. Lakes are bodies of water with land on all sides.

1. ☑ **Reading Check** Main Idea and Details **Underline** the names of different kinds of land. **Highlight** the names of bodies of water.

lake

Using a Globe

Did you know that Earth is round like a ball? You can use a globe to find different places on Earth. A globe shows all of Earth's land and water. Blue stands for water.

You can not see all of Earth at once on a globe. You might have to spin a globe to find the United States!

2. ☑ Reading Check **Look** at the globe. **Point** to water. **Point** to land.

mountains

plains

river

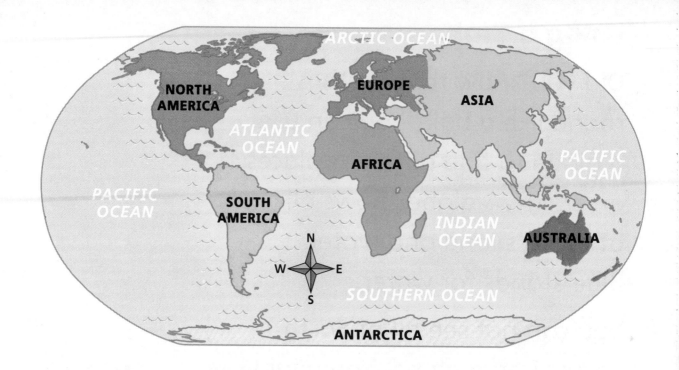

Using a World Map

A map of the world shows all of Earth. It shows Earth's oceans and continents. An **ocean** is a large body of salty water and a **continent** is a large area of land. There are seven continents on Earth. They are North America, South America, Europe, Africa, Asia, Australia, and Antarctica. The United States, Canada, and Mexico are part of North America.

3. ☑Reading Check **Look** at the map. **Circle** the continent where the United States is located.

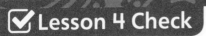 **Lesson 4 Check**

4. Compare and Contrast Write how a map and globe are similar and different.

Similar: _____

_____

_____

_____

Different: _____

_____

_____

5. Draw a picture. **Show** a kind of land and body of water you read about. **Label** each one.

6. Use a separate sheet of paper. **Draw** a map of the world. **Label** your town or city, your state, the United States, the continents, and oceans. Then point to these places on a globe.

Unlock The BIG Question

I will know how weather, location, and the environment affect the way people live.

INTERACTIVITY

Participate in a class discussion to preview the content of this lesson.

Vocabulary

weather
environment
conservation

Academic Vocabulary

consume

JumpStart Activity

Tell about foods you eat, clothing you wear, and your activities.

Weather

The **weather** of a place is what it is like outside. Weather changes every day. It can be sunny and warm in the morning, then rainy and cool at night. The weather can affect what you wear and do. If it is warm, you may wear a swimsuit and go surfing. If it is cool out, you may wear a jacket and ride your bike.

Location

Your location, or where you live, can change what you do, too. Some people live near harbors, or bodies of water near shore. Here it can be very warm. People may work shipping goods to faraway places. They may also kayak for fun. Others live near mountains. They may drive to nearby cities for work. In the mountains, the air can be cool. People here may go rock climbing for fun.

1. ☑ **Reading Check** **Cause and Effect Circle** how weather and location can affect you.

Quest Connection

What activities can people do in or near a harbor?

INTERACTIVITY

Learn more about harbors.

Word Wise

Context Clues

Look for words that help to define *natural resources*.

Academic Vocabulary

consume •
to use up

Environment

The **environment** is the air, weather, land, water, and living things in a place. The environment can affect what people build homes and buildings with and what people grow. Fresh fruits and vegetables grow well in places like California, Washington, Florida, and Georgia.

Conservation is the protection of our land, water, and plants. We are careful not to **consume** too many natural resources. We need water to grow our food. Trees help keep the air clean.

2. 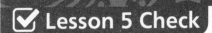**Reading Check** **Look** at the picture. **Tell** what is grown and sold.

Lesson 5 Check

3. Turn and **talk** to a partner. What activities do you do when it is warm outside? What do you do when it is cold?

4. Write how the weather or your location affects what you wear.

_____

_____

_____

_____

_____

_____

5. Understand the *Quest* Connection **Tell** why people can do outdoor activities at a harbor.

Summarize

When you summarize what you read, you use your own words to tell about it. The main idea is the most important idea. Details tell more about the main idea.

Read the paragraph. The main idea is underlined. The details are highlighted. Then read the summary.

New York's Hudson River

People want the Hudson River to be clean. One group teaches others ways they can help the river. Another group dug out the harmful parts at the bottom of the river.

Summary

Groups are working to keep the Hudson River clean.

Your Turn!

1. Read the paragraph.
Underline the main idea.
Highlight the details.

INTERACTIVITY

Review and practice what you learned about how to summarize.

Hudson River Park

Visitors can have lots of fun on the water at the Hudson River Park. They can swim or learn to fish. They can paddle a canoe or a kayak. Visitors can even take a water taxi!

2. Write a summary of the paragraph.
Use your own words.

_____

_____

_____

_____

_____

_____

_____

**Quality:
Courage**

The Corps of Discovery
Explorers

In 1804, Meriwether Lewis, William Clark, and their group set out to find a water route to the Pacific Ocean. They were called the Corps of Discovery. One of the guides was Sacagawea, a Shoshone Indian.

The trip took courage! The group had to take care of any sick members and find enough food. They also had to find their way. They did not always know which direction to go.

Circle how Lewis, Clark, and Sacagawea showed courage.

Talk and Share

Tell about a time when you showed courage.

☑ Assessment

🎮 GAMES

Play the vocabulary game.

Vocabulary and Key Ideas

1. Locate your community on a map.
Describe its **relative location**.

_____

_____

_____

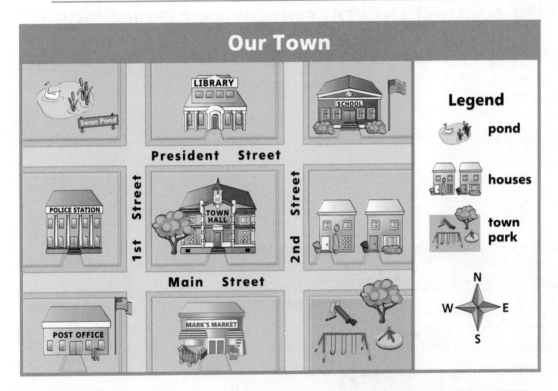

Our Town

LIBRARY   SCHOOL

Swan Pond

President   Street

POLICE STATION   TOWN HALL

1st Street   2nd Street

Main   Street

POST OFFICE   MARK'S MARKET

Legend
🦢 pond
🏠 houses
🌳 town park

N
W ✦ E
S

2. Write whether this is a **map** or a **model**.
Tell why the **legend** is helpful.

_____

_____

_____

3. Write why your state is a great place to live.
Use words like **location**, **weather**, or **environment**.

_____

_____

_____

Critical Thinking and Writing

4. Write a question you can answer by looking at the map. Then ask your question to a partner.

_____

_____

_____

Georgia

Tennessee

North Carolina

N

W — E

S

Alabama

• Dalton

South Carolina

⊙ Atlanta

• Macon

Scale
0   100 mi
0   100 km

Savannah •

Legend

Valdosta

ATLANTIC OCEAN

⊙ state capital

• other city

Florida

Quest Findings

INTERACTIVITY

Use this activity to help you prepare to make your tour guide and map.

Make Your Tour Guide and Map
It's time to put it all together to make your tour guide and map.

Tina

1 Prepare to Write
Work with a partner. What fun activities can people do on land and in water? What interesting places will you write about?

2 Write a Draft
Write about the tour location, weather, and environment. Tell how it affects people's food, clothing, and shelter. Tell about activities and transportation, too.

3 Revise Your Draft
Make changes to your tour guide. Check your spelling and the words you used.

4 Draw a Map
Draw a map of places to visit. Include a title, compass rose, and legend.

5 Present and Perform
Share your tour guide and map. Then act out fun things people can do when they visit!

GO ONLINE FOR DIGITAL RESOURCES

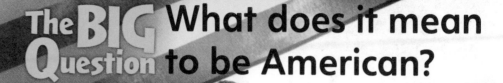

▶ VIDEO

👆 INTERACTIVITY

🔊 AUDIO

🎮 GAMES

☑ ASSESSMENT

📖 eTEXT

The BIG Question

What does it mean to be American?

▶ VIDEO

Jumpstart Activity

👆 INTERACTIVITY

Act out these ways to honor the flag:

1. Put your hand over your heart.
2. Take off your hat and put your hat over your heart.
3. Say the Pledge of Allegiance.

You're a Grand Old Flag

by George M. Cohan

Preview the chapter **vocabulary** by singing "You're a Grand Old Flag."

You're a grand old flag,

You're a high flying flag

And forever in peace may
you wave.

You're the emblem of the land
I love,

The home of the free and
the brave.

Quest
Project-Based Learning

Help Ryan Show Our America

Quest Kick Off

I'm Ryan! I have a pen pal in Japan named Hiro. I am making an *Our America* scrapbook to send him. It should show our country's symbols, traditions, and people. Can you make a page for me?

United States

1 Start with a Brainstorm

Pick a symbol, tradition, or person that you think Hiro should know. Ask yourself these questions: *Why is this important to Americans? What important events are related to this idea or person?* Write down your answers.

INTERACTIVITY
Go online to see more about our symbols, traditions, and people.

2 Look for *Quest* Connections

Turn to the next page to begin looking for Quest Connections that will help you make the scrapbook.

3 Write Up Your *Quest* Findings

Use the Quest Findings page at the end of the chapter to help you make the scrapbook.

Unlock The BIG Question

I will know why the United States flag is important.

INTERACTIVITY

Participate in a class discussion to preview the content of this lesson.

Vocabulary

flag
pledge
tradition
freedom
justice

Academic Vocabulary

brainstorms

JumpStart Activity

Turn to a partner. Talk about what you think it means to make and keep a promise.

Stars and Stripes

Marco and his class stand and face the flag each day. A **flag** is a piece of cloth with colors and patterns. Our flag is the symbol of our country. The United States flag has stars and stripes.

A Promise to Our Country

Marco's class is saying the Pledge of Allegiance. A **pledge** is a promise to be loyal to our country. The Pledge of Allegiance is a **tradition**, or something passed down over time.

1. ☑ Reading Check **Practice** the Pledge of Allegiance. **Take turns** saying it to a partner.

A Promise of Freedom

Academic Vocabulary

brainstorms
• comes up with a lot of ideas

The flag means many things to Americans. Marco's class **brainstorms** a list of meanings. For one thing, the flag stands for freedom. **Freedom** is the ability to do as one wants.

2. ☑Reading Check **Think** about what our flag means to you. **Complete** the chart with a word.

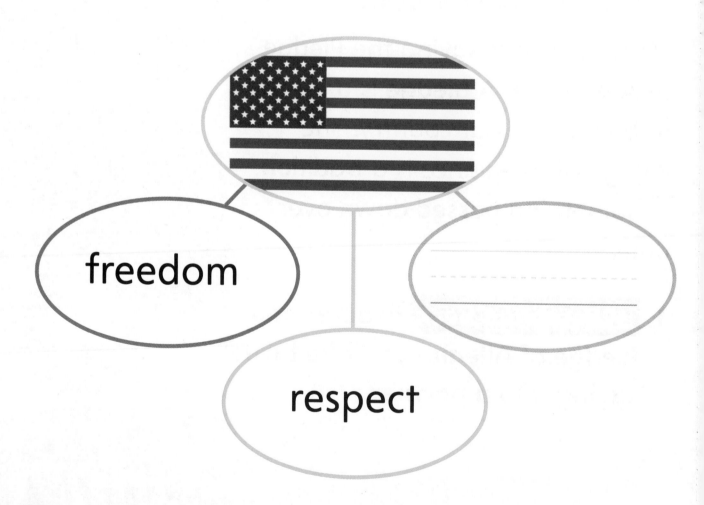

A Promise of Justice

Our flag also stands for justice.
Justice means fair treatment.
The rules of our country are fair.
They say everyone must be treated
the same way.

INTERACTIVITY

Check your understanding
of the key ideas of this
lesson.

☑ Lesson 1 Check

3. Cause and Effect Fill in the box.

Cause		Effect
Marco and his class show _____ _____ _____ for our flag.	→	They show respect for others.

4. The Pledge of Allegiance is a promise to be loyal.
Tell a partner how you are a loyal friend.

5. Tell why our flag is important.

Unlock
The **BIG** Question

I will know about important American symbols.

INTERACTIVITY

Participate in a class discussion to preview the content of this lesson.

Vocabulary

national
emblem
landmark

Academic Vocabulary

symbolizes

JumpStart Activity

Find one thing in your classroom that stands for something. Tell a partner about it.

Why Are Symbols Important?

Our country has many symbols. A symbol stands for a shared idea. Our country's symbols connect us to each other. They connect us to our country's past. The symbol of Uncle Sam is more than 150 years old.

1. ☑ **Reading Check** **Underline** the reasons symbols are important to Americans.

Our National Bird

Animals can be symbols. The bald eagle is America's national bird. **National** means something belonging to a nation. The bald eagle is an **emblem**, or symbol, of freedom. The bald eagle shows that America is strong. It is on our money. The eagle is also part of our nation's seal, or stamp.

2. ☑ **Reading Check** Use **Evidence From Text Fill in the blank. The bald eagle is on our nation's seal and our**

_____

_____ .

Quest Connection

Underline why the bald eagle is an American symbol.

👆 INTERACTIVITY

Learn more about the symbols you could use in your Quest.

Word Wise

Compound Words

What two words make up the word *landmark*?

Academic Vocabulary

symbolizes • stands for

Gifts can become symbols. In 1885, the people of France gave Americans a gift. It was a copper statue more than 150 feet tall. Today, the Statue of Liberty is a famous **landmark** in New York Harbor. A landmark is a famous thing that is well known. The statue **symbolizes** freedom.

3. ☑ **Reading Check**

Circle the torch in the Statue of Liberty's hand. **Tell** a partner how the torch might help boats.

The Golden Gate Bridge

A state landmark can be a national symbol. The Golden Gate Bridge stands for our creativity. People said it was not possible to build a bridge that long. American engineers did not give up. They built a bridge across San Francisco Bay.

INTERACTIVITY

Check your understanding of the key ideas of this lesson.

☑ Lesson 2 Check

4. **Circle true** or **false** about the following sentence: Symbols connect Americans to our country's past.

5. **Fill in** the blank. The Statue of Liberty was a gift from

_____

_____ .

6. **Understand the** *Quest* Connection **Choose** a symbol from this lesson. **Turn** and **talk** to a partner about why it is important to Americans.

Cause and Effect

Elei was practicing her batting. She hit the ball the wrong way. It broke a window in her house!

A cause is what makes something happen. What caused the ball to break the window? Elei hit it the wrong way.

An effect is what happens. What effect did it have when Elei hit the ball the wrong way? It broke a window.

Your Turn!

The first United States flag had one star for each state. Over time, the flag changed as more states joined.

INTERACTIVITY

Review and practice what you learned about cause and effect.

1777   **Today**

1. **Think** about what caused the flag to change. How did it change? **Fill in** the boxes.

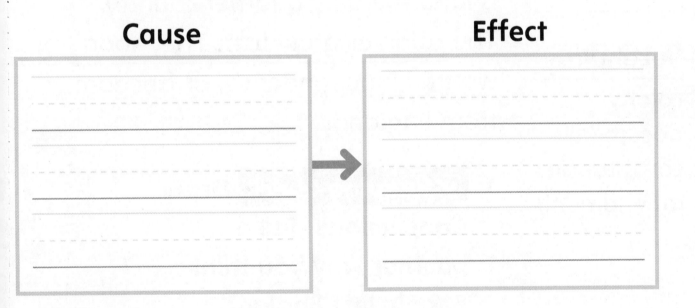

Cause   **Effect**

2. **Work** with a partner. **Talk** about another cause and effect.

Unlock
The BIG
Question

I will know about important American documents.

INTERACTIVITY

Participate in a class discussion to preview the content of this lesson.

Vocabulary

colony
document
constitution
amendments

JumpStart Activity

Talk with a partner about why we sometimes write down ideas on paper.

Building Colonies

Long ago, people came here from England. They built colonies. A **colony** is land ruled by another country. The colonies grew fast. They soon wanted independence, or freedom, from England.

1. ☑ **Reading Check** **Draw Conclusions** **Tell** a partner why you think people left England.

The Declaration of Independence

On July 4, 1776, leaders of the colonies approved a **document**, or a piece of paper with important information. It was called the Declaration of Independence. It said the colonies were free. In it, Thomas Jefferson wrote, "All men are created equal."

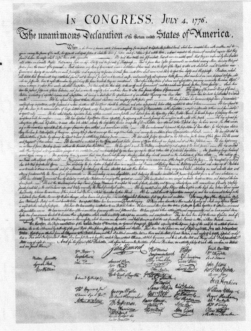

2. ☑ **Reading Check** Main Idea and Details **Underline** details about the Declaration of Independence.

The U.S. Constitution

England fought a war to keep the colonies. The colonists won their freedom. Then the leaders wrote the Constitution of the United States. A **constitution** is a written set of laws. Our Constitution lists the laws of our government.

Over time, **amendments**, or changes, were made. Leaders added rules to protect our rights. The first ten changes to the Constitution are known as the Bill of Rights.

3. ☑ Reading Check **Circle what the Constitution lists.**

The First Amendment of the Bill of Rights

 You are free to meet to talk about the government.

You are free to practice any religion.

You are free to speak about your own ideas and opinions.

 You are free to write and speak about your own ideas and opinions in newspapers or radio.

INTERACTIVITY

Check your understanding of the key ideas of this lesson.

☑ Lesson 3 Check

4. Cause and Effect Why was the Declaration of Independence approved?

_____

_____

_____

5. What did the colonists give up? What did they get in return?

_____

_____

_____

6. Tell how our Constitution changed.

Lesson 4 American Songs

Unlock The BIG Question

I will know about important American songs.

INTERACTIVITY

Participate in a class discussion to preview the content of this lesson.

Vocabulary

anthem
grand

JumpStart Activity

Sing a favorite song for a partner. Tell why it is important to you.

Our National Anthem

In 1814, America was at war with England. British ships attacked Fort McHenry. The battle lasted all night. An American named Francis Scott Key was there. He watched the American flag on the fort. It was still there at dawn. We had won!

Francis wrote that the flag waved "Over the land of the free, And the home of the brave." His words are now a song. It is our national anthem, "The Star-Spangled Banner." An **anthem** is a song of praise. Singing our national anthem is a tradition. It is sung at schools and sports games.

1. ☑️**Reading Check** **Main Idea and Details** **Underline** the name of our national anthem. **Circle** the name of the person who wrote it.

My Country, 'Tis of Thee

Quest Connection

Highlight why Dr. Smith wrote "My Country, 'Tis of Thee."

Another American song is "My Country, 'Tis of Thee." Dr. Samuel Francis Smith wrote the song in 1831. He wrote it for school children. He wanted them to honor our past and give thanks for our freedom.

2.  Reading Check **Learn** the words to "My Country, 'Tis of Thee." **Work** with a partner to make dance moves for it.

INTERACTIVITY

Learn more about the American songs you could use in your Quest.

You're a Grand Old Flag

"You're a Grand Old Flag" is also an American song that we sing. George M. Cohan wrote it in 1906. He said that the flag was **grand**, or important. The song shows love for America.

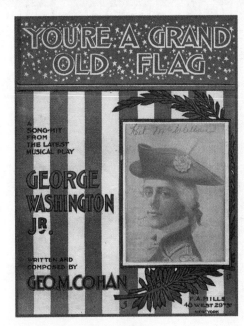

3. 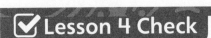 **Sing** "You're a Grand Old Flag" with a partner.

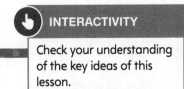

INTERACTIVITY

Check your understanding of the key ideas of this lesson.

☑ Lesson 4 Check

4. **Cause and Effect Circle** the correct answer. Francis Scott Key saw our flag flying after a battle. His words are now a book / song.

5. **Tell** a partner why you sing traditional songs.

6. **Understand the** *Quest* **Connection** Many songs use rhymes. Rhyming can help you remember words. **Write** two words that rhyme in one of the songs in this lesson.

_____

_____

"My Country, 'Tis of Thee"

"My Country, 'Tis of Thee" is a primary source. It tells about our country.

Vocabulary Support

this is about you

about you

our country's early settlers and soldiers

our country's first settlers

liberty • freedom

pride • a feeling of joy after a hard task

My country, 'tis of thee,
Sweet land of liberty,
Of thee I sing:
Land where my fathers died,
Land of the pilgrim's pride,
From every mountain side,
Let freedom ring.

– Dr. Samuel Francis Smith

Fun Fact

"My Country, 'Tis of Thee" is sung to the tune of England's national anthem.

Dr. Samuel Francis Smith

Using a Primary Source

1. Circle the words that show love for our country's right to be free.

2. Draw a box around the words that remember the Americans who came before us.

3. Turn to a partner. **Ask** a question about the song.

Wrap It Up

Summarize Tell your teacher what the song says about our country.

5 American Heroes

The BIG Question

I will know about important American heroes.

🖐 **INTERACTIVITY**

Participate in a class discussion to preview the content of this lesson.

Vocabulary

hero
migrant
worker

Academic Vocabulary

demonstrations

JumpStart Activity

Draw a poster of someone you look up to. Tell the class about him or her.

What Is a Hero?

Our country has heroes. A **hero** is someone who works hard to help others. Some heroes keep us safe and healthy. Others make our rules fair. Many holidays honor American heroes.

1. ☑ **Reading Check** **Underline things our heroes do.**

Heroes for Freedom

George Washington is an American hero. He led our country's first army.

George Washington

He helped America become free and was our first president.

Harriet Tubman was a hero for freedom, too. At the time, many African Americans were not free. She helped lead them to freedom. She did this even though she had a disability that made her fall asleep without warning.

Harriet Tubman

2. ☑ Reading Check **Circle** the name of an American hero. **Highlight** an example of how this hero helped our country.

Dr. Martin Luther King, Jr.

César Chávez

Heroes for Justice

Dr. Martin Luther King, Jr. is an American hero. Dr. King believed in justice for all. He led peaceful **demonstrations**. He worked to change unfair laws. Dr. King made sure African Americans could vote.

Academic Vocabulary

demonstrations
• public meetings or marches against something that is not right

3. ☑ Reading Check Summarize **Tell a partner why Dr. King is an important American hero.**

César Chávez is an American hero.
He spent his life helping migrant workers.
A **migrant worker** moves from place
to place for work. At the time, migrant
workers were not treated fairly. César led
demonstrations to change the unfair laws.

INTERACTIVITY

Check your understanding
of the key ideas of this
lesson.

☑ Lesson 5 Check

4. **Cause and Effect Finish** the sentence.
   Dr. Martin Luther King, Jr. and César Chávez
   changed people's lives by helping to make our
   country's laws more

   _____

   _____

   _____ .

5. **Tell** a partner why we remember heroes
   from America's past.

6. **Tell** a partner about some ways a person
   can be a hero.

Analyze Images

You can analyze images. To analyze is to look closely. Ask questions about what you see.

President Barack Obama greets children in Washington, D.C.

1

Location

2

President Barack Obama greets children in Washington, D.C.

Caption

3

People

"Where is this place? What kind of place is it?"

"What does the caption say?" The caption is the sentence under the image.

"Do the people look happy or sad? What is happening?"

Look closely at the image below.

👆 INTERACTIVITY

Review and practice what you learned about analyzing images.

Children join an Independence Day parade.

1. Circle the kind of place this image shows.

a school   a town   a home

2. Underline the words in the caption that say what these people are celebrating.

3. Draw a box around an American symbol in the image.

4. Write a sentence to tell how you think the children in the image feel.

_____

_____

_____

_____

Lesson 6 Our National Holidays

Unlock The BIG Question

I will know about important national holidays.

INTERACTIVITY

Participate in a class discussion to preview the content of this lesson.

Vocabulary

veteran
armed
 forces
memorial

Academic Vocabulary

military

JumPstart Activity

Act out a holiday tradition from home. Have a partner guess what holiday it is.

What Is a Holiday?

Our holidays honor people and events. Presidents' Day honors George Washington and Abraham Lincoln. We celebrate Independence Day every July 4th.

1. ✓ **Reading Check** **Look** at the picture. **Ask** and **answer** questions about it with a partner.

A Time to Give Thanks

Thanksgiving is an American holiday. It honors the first Pilgrim harvest. The Pilgrims were early American colonists. American Indians showed them how to live off the land. To thank them, the Pilgrims shared a harvest dinner.

Quest Connection

Circle why Thanksgiving is an important holiday for Americans.

👆 **INTERACTIVITY**

Learn more about holidays you could use in your Quest.

2. ☑ **Reading Check** Draw Conclusions **Tell** about one way that Thanksgiving connects us to our past.

A Time to Honor and Remember

Memorial Day and Veterans Day both honor our armed forces. A **veteran** is a man or woman who served in the armed forces. The **armed forces** are all the soldiers who protect a country.

On these holidays, people show their respect. People put flags on **military** graves and memorials. A **memorial** is something people build to honor a person or event.

3. ☑ **Reading Check** **Draw something you might do on Memorial Day.**

Academic Vocabulary

military • having to do with soldiers

Honoring Equal Rights

Other holidays honor Americans who worked for equal rights. Martin Luther King, Jr. Day is in January. On this holiday, we remember and honor the work he did.

✓ Lesson 6 Check

4. Ask and **answer** a question about Veterans Day.

_____

_____

_____

_____

5. Finish the sentence. American holidays honor

_____

_____ and _____.

6. Understand the *Quest* Connection **Talk** with a partner. **Describe** an American symbol that could teach people about Independence Day.

★ Citizenship

**Quality:
Commitment**

Susan B. Anthony
Hero for Women's Rights

Years ago, only American men could vote. Susan B. Anthony wanted the laws to be fair. Susan gave many speeches and talked to leaders. She said women should be able to vote, too. She spent many years working for this change. Later, in 1920, women won the right to vote.

Draw a picture of Susan B. Anthony working for the right to vote.

Show Your Commitment

Tell about a time when you did not give up and showed a commitment to something.

SUSAN B. A
HEADQUARTER

Cultural Heritage

☑ **Assessment**

🎮 **GAMES**

Play the vocabulary game.

Vocabulary and Key Ideas

1. Fill in the circle next to the best answers. Which items below are **national** symbols?

Ⓐ   Ⓑ   Ⓒ   Ⓓ

2. Main Idea and Details Pick a symbol from question 1. **Write** a sentence about what it stands for.

_____

_____

_____

_____

_____

3. Look at the pictures. **Circle** any pictures that show an American tradition. **Underline** any that do not.

Critical Thinking and Writing

4. Look at the American heroes.
Write their names below their pictures.
Tell a partner why they are **heroes**.

_____

_____

Quest Findings

⏺ **INTERACTIVITY**
Use this activity to help you prepare to make your scrapbook page.

Write Your Scrapbook Page
It's time to help Ryan make the *Our America* scrapbook for Hiro!

1 **Get Ready to Write**
What do you want to say and show about America? Remember, Ryan wants to tell Hiro how symbols and traditions connect Americans.

2 **Write and Draw**
Tell details about your choice. What or who is it? Why is it important to America?

3 **Put It Together**
Give your page to your teacher. Make a cover for your class book.

4 **Show Your Class**
Show your page to the class. Tell everyone about your drawing. Read to them what you wrote.

Chapter

4

Life Today and Long Ago

GO ONLINE FOR DIGITAL RESOURCES

 VIDEO

 INTERACTIVITY

 AUDIO

 GAMES

 ASSESSMENT

 eTEXT

The BIG Question

How does life change throughout history?

▶ VIDEO

JumpStart Activity

👆 INTERACTIVITY

Take turns with a partner. Tell how you have changed over time.

110

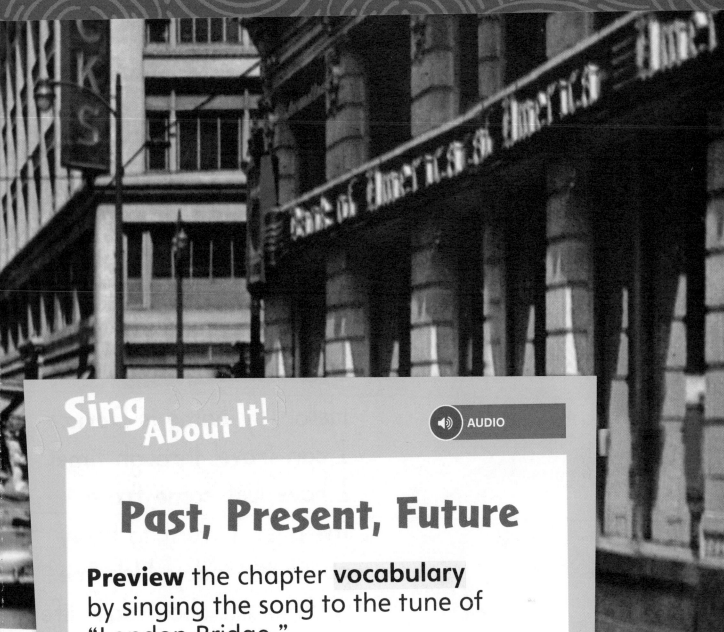

🔊 AUDIO

Past, Present, Future

Preview the chapter **vocabulary**
by singing the song to the tune of
"London Bridge."

The **present**, **past**, and **future** are
displayed on a **calendar**.
In our recent **history**
there were changes in **technology**.

111

Quest
Project-Based Learning

Help Daria the Time Traveler!

Quest Kick Off

Hello! My name is Daria. I can travel through time! I have just come from the past. I want to know about life today. Help me write a skit about daily life now and long ago. Then have fun acting out the skit!

1 Start with a Brainstorm

Think about something that is different from long ago. Are clothing and games the same? Has school changed? Draw a picture to show something that has changed over time.

INTERACTIVITY

Learn more about life now and long ago.

2 Look for Quest Connections

Turn to the next page to begin looking for Quest Connections. They will help you write and act out your skit.

3 Write Up Your Quest Findings

Use the Quest Findings page at the end of the chapter to help you write a skit. Show and tell what has changed and what has stayed the same. Then act it out!

I will know ways we can measure time.

> 👆 **INTERACTIVITY**
>
> Participate in a class discussion to preview the content of this lesson.

Vocabulary

present
past
future
calendar

Academic Vocabulary

measure

JumpStart Activity

Make a chart with a partner. Write the words *Day* and *Night* at the top. Tell what you do during these times.

Talking About Time

The **present** is today. *Now* tells about the present. The **past** is what happened before. *Then* tells about the past. The **future** is what will happen later. *Tomorrow* tells about the future.

1. ☑ **Reading Check** Main Idea and Details **Underline** words we use to talk about time.

A Clock Tells Time

A clock helps us tell time. Clocks show the time of day or night. Some clocks have hands to show the minutes and hours. Other clocks use numbers.

2. ☑**Reading Check** **Draw** a picture of a clock. **Show** what time it is now.

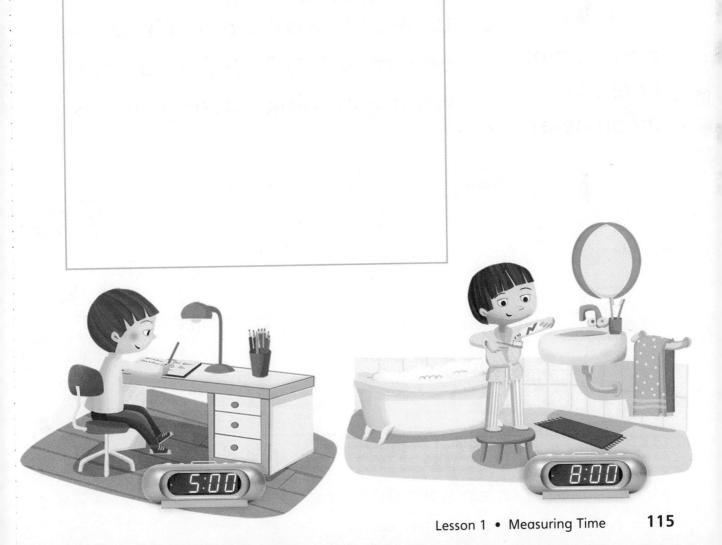

Academic Vocabulary

measure • to find out the size or amount of something

Word Wise

Multiple Meanings

Row means "to move a boat using oars." What does *row* mean here?

A Calendar Measures Time

A **calendar** shows the days, weeks, and months of the year. It helps us keep track of, or **measure**, time.

A calendar is a chart with rows and boxes. The name of the month is at the top. The days of the week are in the first row. There is a day in each box.

3. ☑️**Reading Check** Sequence **Look** at the calendar. **Circle** the day after July 3. **Tell** a partner what you think the flag stands for.

JULY calendar

	Sunday	Monday	Tuesday	Wednesday	Thursday	Friday	Saturday
		1	2	3	4	5	6
	7	8	9	10	11	12	13
	14	15	16	17	18	19	20
	21	22	23	24	25	26	27
	28	29	30	31			

☑ Lesson 1 Check

4. Compare and Contrast What two tools help you measure time? **Tell** how they are similar and different.

5. Finish the sentence.

When you keep track of time, you _____ it.

6. Draw yourself in the past. **Draw** yourself now. **Tell** about your pictures.

Interpret Timelines

A timeline shows the order of events. You read a timeline from left to right. The earliest event is on the left. The latest event is on the right.

This timeline shows how Aiden changed over time. It shows how some things stayed the same, too.

What happened in 2012? First, find that year on the timeline. Put your finger on that year. Then, look at the picture and read the sentence below 2012.

2012	2014	2016	Present
I was born.	I turned two.	My sister Malia was born.	I started first grade.

1. Look at the timeline. **Circle** the picture of Aiden in the present. **Underline** the event.

2. Look at the timeline. What stayed the same from 2012 to the present?

_____

_____

_____

_____

3. Look at the timeline. **Draw** your own timeline to show your life.

2 Schools and Communities Past and Present

Unlock The BIG Question

I will know how schools and communities have changed over time and how they have stayed the same.

INTERACTIVITY

Participate in a class discussion to preview the content of this lesson.

Vocabulary

history
century
generation

Academic Vocabulary

decade

JumpStart Activity

Tell a partner what kindergarten was like. Tell how first grade is different.

What Is History?

History is the story of the past. It tells about people, places, and events. Some things do change over time. Other things stay the same.

1. ☑ **Reading Check** Main Idea and Details **Circle** what history tells us about.

Schools Past and Present

Long ago, many American children learned in a school with one room. Today, most children learn in big schools with many classrooms.

Long ago, most children walked to school. Today, many children in the United States ride on a school bus. In some parts of the world, children ride boats to get to school!

Word Wise

Compound Words

What smaller words make up the big word *classrooms*?

2. ☑ **Reading Check** Compare and Contrast **Tell** a partner one thing that is the same about schools in different places. **Tell** one thing that is different.

| 1800s | 2000s |

Academic Vocabulary

decade • a ten year period

Quest Connection

How do communities change over time? How do they stay the same?

👆 **INTERACTIVITY**

Learn more about how to show schools and communities in the past and present.

Communities Grow

Around the world, places change over each **decade** and century. A decade is ten years. A **century** is 100 years. Over time, people build new buildings. People start new businesses.

Many generations of people live in a community. A **generation** means people who were born at about the same time.

3. ☑ **Reading Check** **Look** at the timeline. **Circle** the community from the 1800s.

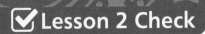

✓ Lesson 2 Check

4. Ask and Answer Questions Write a question and answer it. **Tell** how school is different today from long ago.

_____

_____

_____

_____

5. Finish each sentence. **Write** the correct word on each line.

A _____ means 100 years.

A _____ means ten years.

6. Understand the _Quest_ **Connection** **Draw** two pictures on a separate sheet of paper. **Label** each picture _Then_ or _Now_. **Show** one way a community changes over time.

Daily Life Past and Present

Unlock The BIG Question

I will know how daily life has changed over time and how it has stayed the same.

INTERACTIVITY

Participate in a class discussion to preview the content of this lesson.

Vocabulary

manners
festival

Academic Vocabulary

general

JumpStart Activity

Take turns with a partner. Act out jobs that people do today.

People at Work Long Ago

Daily life was different in the past. Long ago, many people worked on farms. They planted crops by hand.

Many people worked in the home. They sewed their own clothes. They cooked their own food.

People at Work Today

Today, many people around the world work in cities. Some jobs are in office buildings. Other jobs are in stores and homes.

Some people who work in the home still sew and cook. Others use computers to work.

1. ☑ **Reading Check** Main Idea and Details **Underline** ways in which work today is different from work long ago.

Clothing

Clothing can change over time. Long ago, American girls wore long dresses. Boys wore long shorts and tall socks. Today, children may wear jeans and T-shirts.

At times, clothing stays the same. In Peru, some children still wear traditional capes.

2. ☑ **Reading Check** **Circle** the **United States on the map. Tell** how American clothing has changed.

Manners

Daily life has **general** rules.
One rule is to use good manners.
Manners are the ways we are polite.
Long ago, American children bowed
to say hello or goodbye. Today, many
children wave instead.

Manners can be different around
the world. African Maasai children
tilt their heads to say hello.

3. ☑ **Reading Check** **Underline**
good manners.

Festivals

Festivals are a part of daily life. A **festival** is a special time. Cities in New York, Washington, and Idaho all have Scottish festivals. People play Scottish games from long ago.

The Mid-Autumn Moon Festival is from China. It began because of folklore, or stories, about the moon. Many families today celebrate it with food rather than stories.

4. ☑ **Reading Check** Cause and Effect **Underline** the reason why one festival began.

Quest Connection

How is life today different from the past? How is it the same?

👆 **INTERACTIVITY**

Learn more about how to show daily life in the past and present.

5. Compare and Contrast Write how one festival today is different from the past.

_____

_____

_____

_____

6. Ask and **answer** a question about something you learned in this lesson.

_____

_____

_____

_____

_____

_____

7. Understand the *Quest* Connection **Draw** a picture. **Show** how work, clothing, or festivals were different in the past. **Tell** a classmate how things are the same.

Compare and Contrast

We compare to show how things are similar, or alike. We contrast to show how things are different, or not the same.

Look at the pictures. How are they similar? How are they different?

Children in the past had fun bowling.

Children like bowling today, too. We can now play bowling on a video game.

Your Turn!

Review and practice what you learned about how to compare and contrast.

INTERACTIVITY

Review and practice what you learned about comparing and contrasting.

1. Look at the bowling pictures. **Tell** more about how the pictures are similar and different.

2. Look at the hockey pictures. **Write** how these games are similar and different.

_____

_____

_____

_____

Changes in Technology and Transportation

I will know how technology and transportation have changed over time.

👆 **INTERACTIVITY**

Participate in a class discussion to preview the content of this lesson.

Vocabulary

invention
technology
communicate
transportation

JumpStart Activity

Work with a partner. Make a list of things you use that make your life easier.

Inventions

An **invention** is something that is made for the first time. Inventions make life easier. Long ago, people washed clothing by hand. Today, many people use washing machines.

1. ☑**Reading Check** Main Idea and Details **Look** at the pictures. **Circle** an invention.

Technology

Technology has changed from the past. Technology is the use of science to solve problems. It has changed how we **communicate**, or share information with others.

Long ago, people wrote letters. It took weeks for a letter to travel by horse and rider. Today, we have cell phones. We can send e-mail. An e-mail is sent on a computer.

2. ☑ Reading Check **Underline words that tell about technology we use today.**

Quest **Connection**

How has technology made people's lives easier?

👆 INTERACTIVITY

Learn more in the Museum of Technology.

Transportation

Transportation is the way people move from place to place. Long ago, people walked or rode horses. Later, ships and trains were invented. Transportation was still slow.

Today, people travel fast. We use cars, buses, and subways. One bullet train in Japan can go almost 200 miles per hour!

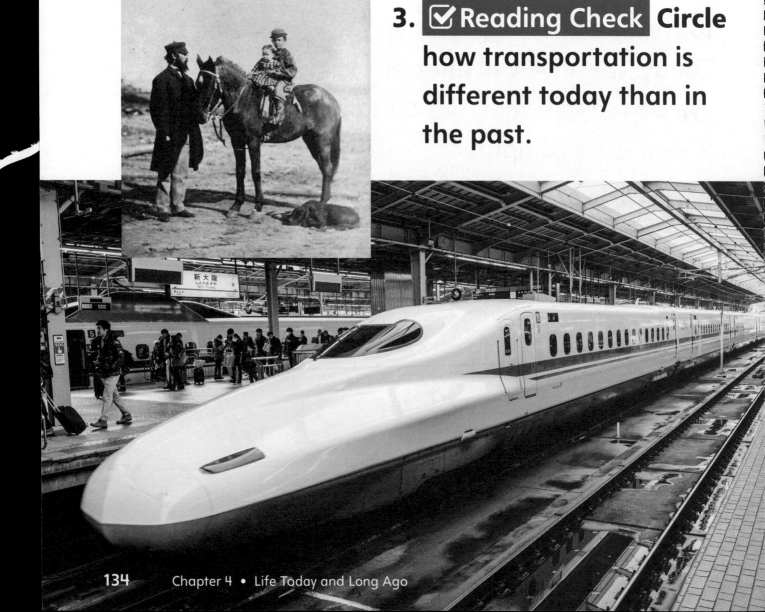

3. ☑**Reading Check** **Circle how transportation is different today than in the past.**

☑ Lesson 4 Check

4. Compare and Contrast Write how transportation today is similar to and different from the past.

_____

_____

_____

_____

_____

5. Work with a partner. **Ask** and **answer** questions about transportation, communication, and technology.

6. Understand the *Quest* Connection **Draw** a picture. **Show** an invention that is used in schools today.

Juliette Gordon Low on Forming the Girl Guides

Juliette Gordon Low was born in Savannah, Georgia. In 1911, she wrote a letter to her father. She wrote of her plan to start a guide, or scouting, group for girls in Scotland. Soon after, she started a group in Savannah. This group is now known as the Girl Scouts of America.

Vocabulary Support

a long, deep valley ·············

high land with ·····················
mountains

activities done for fun ··········

"I am getting up a Corp of Girl Guides here in this <u>Glen</u> where the <u>highland</u> girls are so far from the world . . . I like girls, I like this organization and the rules and <u>pastimes</u>, so if you find that I get very deeply interested you must not be surprised!"

Juliette Gordon Low (center)

Using a Primary Source

1. Read the letter. **Write** where the girls lived.

_____

_____

_____

_____

2. Underline what Low liked about the guide group.

Wrap It Up

Summarize what you learned about Low. Then write what fun activities you like to do.

_____

_____

_____

_____

_____

_____

_____

_____

Quality:
Respect for the rights of others

Ruby Bridges
A Brave Girl

In the 1960s, some people did not want African American children and white children to go to school together. Ruby Bridges was one of the first African American children to go to a school of only white children. Some people blocked her way and took their children out of the school. Today, all children can go to the same schools.

"I spent the whole year in an empty classroom with just my teacher."

—Ruby Bridges

Tell how people wanted to respect people's rights.

Talk and Share

Tell how you respect the rights of others.

☑ Assessment

Vocabulary and Key Ideas

1. Write about the **invention** of the washing machine. Finish the sentence.

It makes people's lives easier because

_____

_____

_____ .

2. Write the word that comes next.

past, _____ , **future**

3. Draw a picture of the clothing people wore in the past.

4. Look at the timeline of <mark>transportation</mark>. **Draw** a picture of a plane in the box for 2017. **Circle** the earliest date on the timeline.

| 1896 | 1920 | 2017 |

Critical Thinking and Writing

5. Look at the pictures. **Write** how some things changed over time. **Write** how some things stayed the same.

_____

_____

_____

_____

_____

Quest Findings

INTERACTIVITY

Use this activity to help you prepare to write your skit.

Write Your Skit

It's time to write your skit!

1 Prepare to Write

Work in a small group to answer the questions. Are clothing and games the same? How has our community changed?

2 Write a Draft

Write a skit. Tell about how things have changed and stayed the same.

3 Revise Your Draft

Make changes to the skit. Check your spelling and the words you used.

4 Practice Your Skit

Assign roles to classmates. Practice your skit.

5 Present and Perform

Share your skit with the class.

Chapter 5
One Nation, Many People

GO ONLINE FOR
DIGITAL RESOURCES

- ▶ VIDEO
- 👆 INTERACTIVITY
- 🔊 AUDIO
- 🎮 GAMES
- ☑ ASSESSMENT
- 📖 eTEXT

The BIG Question

▶ VIDEO

How do so many different people make one nation?

Jumpstart Activity

👆 INTERACTIVITY

Ask your classmates to name the different languages they speak. Make a bar graph to show the number of different languages.

Our America

Preview the chapter **vocabulary** by singing the song to the tune of "Pop Goes the Weasel."

Different **countries** have their own **culture** and **beliefs.**

They **benefit** from having **goals** that help them to **succeed.**

The **immigrants contribute** to our **economy.**

Their **legends** and their **folk tales** are as **clever** as can be.

Create a Flag for Artist Annie!

Quest Kick Off

Hello! My name is Annie. I am an artist. I want to celebrate the different cultures in our state. Can you help me create a culture flag? What symbols can we draw to show all the cultures in our state? Let's work together to create and display our flags!

1 Start with a Brainstorm

Think about symbols that show your culture. *What foods do you eat? What holidays do you celebrate? What clothing do you wear?* Draw pictures that show your culture.

INTERACTIVITY

Explore symbols of different cultures.

2 Look for *Quest* Connections

Turn to the next page to begin looking for your Quest Connections.

3 Write Up Your *Quest* Findings

Use the Quest Findings page at the end of the chapter to help you make your culture flag and write about it.

What Is Culture?

I will know what culture means.

INTERACTIVITY

Participate in a class discussion to preview the content of this lesson.

Vocabulary

countries
culture
beliefs

JumpStart Activity

Turn and talk to a partner. Make a list of things all people need.

How We Are the Same

People come to America from many different **countries**, or nations, from around the world. We all have the same basic needs. We all need food, shelter, and love to grow and stay safe.

1. ☑ **Reading Check** Main Idea and Details **Circle** the things all people need.

How We Are Different

When people came to America, they brought things that were important. These things make up their **culture**. Culture is the way a group of people lives.

People brought their music, food, and dance. They brought their language. They brought their **beliefs**, or things they thought were true, too. There are many different cultures in the United States today.

2. ☑ Reading Check **Look** at the pictures of the two boys and the girl. **Tell** a partner how their traditional clothing is different.

In My Class

Look around your classroom. Your friends and their parents might be from different countries.

Some classes are made up of people from all over the world. Children can learn about different cultures and ways of thinking. Think about how many languages you could hear if you had friends from Mexico, Korea, and India!

Quest Connection

How many languages do you hear when you are at home?

👆 **INTERACTIVITY**

Explore and practice different languages.

3. ☑ **Reading Check** **Turn** and **Talk Tell** what makes your class special.

In My Neighborhood

In some neighborhoods, people from all over the world live together on the same street.

On this street, there are families from Korea, Mexico, and the Philippines. They eat, sing, and play games together. They share their cultures with each other.

INTERACTIVITY

Check your understanding of the key ideas of this lesson.

☑ Lesson 1 Check

4. Tell a partner two things that make up a person's culture.

5. Compare and Contrast Write how people are the same. How are they different?

All people have the same _____.

They do not have the same _____.

6. Understand the *Quest* **Connections Ask** your friends what languages they speak. **Find out** how to say "hello" in another language!

Lesson 2 Customs, Traditions, and Celebrations

Unlock The BIG Question

I will know about customs, traditions, and celebrations.

INTERACTIVITY

Participate in a class discussion to preview the content of this lesson.

Vocabulary

custom

Academic Vocabulary

ceremony

JumPstart Activity

Turn to a partner. Tell about your favorite family celebration.

Customs

A **custom** is something that a person usually does in a certain way. Some customs are passed down over time. Other customs are new. Groups of people from the same place often share the same customs. For example, they probably say hello the same way.

1. ☑**Reading Check** Main Idea and Details **Underline** the words that describe a custom.

Ways People Say Hello They might shake hands, bow, or wave.

Traditions and Celebrations

A tradition is like a custom. It is something that people have passed down over time. Most traditions come from the past. Sometimes, traditions can be new. We can start new traditions.

Everyone follows different traditions. Many people cook special food to celebrate their important holidays. They may dress in traditional clothing to dance and sing at a celebration.

Quest Connection

What are some birthday customs in your family?

INTERACTIVITY

Learn about different birthday celebrations.

Academic Vocabulary

ceremony • a special and important event

Meet Maria

Maria is six years old. She lives in California but was born in Mexico. She came to America when she was three.

Maria's traditions are important to her and her family. This year, Maria's sister will turn 15. This is a special birthday for a Mexican girl! It is called quinceañera. Maria's sister will have a big **ceremony** and a celebration with special food. This ceremony is an important Mexican tradition for many.

Meet Ji-hu

Ji-hu is seven years old. He lives in New York. His parents came here from Korea when they were young.

Korean traditions are very important to Ji-hu and his family. They take their shoes off before they go inside their home. They sit on mats when they eat. Ji-hu's favorite holiday is called Chuseok. He eats special cakes made of rice during this celebration of the fall season.

2. ☑**Reading Check** **Underline one of Ji-hu's traditions.**

Word Wise
Suffixes
The word *celebration* ends in *-tion*. Find another word on the page that ends in *-tion*.

Meet Hopo

Hopo is seven years old. She was born in Samoa, an island in the Pacific Ocean. Hopo lives in Hawaii now with her grandparents.

Samoan traditions are important to Hopo and her family. Hopo has learned how to make a special mat called 'ie tōga. These special mats can take years to make. They are given as gifts during weddings and other special times. They are passed down in families.

3. ☑ **Reading Check** **Tell** how the mats are special.

☑ **Lesson 2 Check**

4. Tell what customs and traditions your family celebrates.

5. Compare Think about how Ji-hu and Maria's cultures are alike. **Think** about how Ji-hu and Hopo's cultures are alike. **Finish** the sentences.

Ji-hu and Maria's cultures are alike because

_____

_____

_____

_____ .

Ji-hu and Hopo's cultures are alike because

_____

_____

_____ .

6. Understand the *Quest* **Connections** What age is a special birthday in your culture? **Draw** a picture of the celebration.

Compare Points of View

Your point of view is what you think or feel about something. Some people will agree with you. Others will not.

Ms. Calva's class went on a field trip to a history museum. They saw a mural that showed people arriving in New York many years ago. The people arriving were from different countries.

Ana and Tyler have different points of view about how the people must have felt.

I think the people felt scared.

I think the people felt excited.

1. Draw a picture to show your point of view. How do you think the people arriving in New York felt?

INTERACTIVITY

Review and practice what you learned about point of view.

2. Does your point of view match Ana's or Tyler's? Or is it different? **Write** about your point of view. **Turn** and **talk** to a partner.

I think the people felt _____

_____

_____

_____ .

Unlock
The **BIG**
Question

I will know how we are all part of the same community.

👆 INTERACTIVITY

Participate in a class discussion to preview the content of this lesson.

Vocabulary

diverse
goals
benefit

Academic Vocabulary

succeed

Jumpstart Activity

Act out how you and your friends work together.

Ms. Figura's Class

This is Ms. Figura's first-grade class. The children are all part of the same community. They work together in large and small groups. They study and learn from each other.

1. **☑Reading Check Tell** how Ms. Figura's class is like your class. **Underline** how the children are part of a community.

Different Cultures

Just like in your class, the children in Ms. Figura's class are **diverse**. The children and their families come from many different countries. Some children speak more than one language. They have different beliefs, customs, and traditions, too.

2. **☑Reading Check Highlight** how the students are different.

We Want the Same Things

Word Wise

Multiple Meanings

Goal means "what we hope to get." What does *goal* mean in sports?

Academic Vocabulary

succeed • do well

In our class, we talk together. We share our ideas because we all want to answer the same questions.

We all share the same **goals**, or what we hope to do or get. We all want to **succeed**. We know that we can succeed if we work together.

Our community is diverse, too. Many of our neighbors come from different countries.

It is not always easy to understand one another. But when you do, you learn about different customs, traditions, and celebrations. We all **benefit**, or have better lives, when we understand where other people come from.

3. ☑ Reading Check **Look** at the pictures. **Circle** the children who are sharing ideas.

INTERACTIVITY

Check your understanding of the key ideas of this lesson.

☑ **Lesson 3 Check**

4. **Compare and Contrast Share** a goal you have with a partner. **Compare** and **contrast** your goal with your partner's.

5. **Solve a Problem** Imagine a new girl from a different country arrives in your class. **Tell** how you can help her feel part of the community.

6. **Finish** the sentence.
My community works together by

_____

- -

_____ .

Unlock The BIG Question

I will know about American Indians.

INTERACTIVITY

Participate in a class discussion to preview the content of this lesson.

Vocabulary

traded
storytelling
oral
folk tales

Academic Vocabulary

practice

JumpStart Activity

Tell what you know about American Indians.

American Indians in the Past

American Indians have lived across the United States. Each cultural group has their own special traditions and celebrations. They have **traded**, or exchanged, goods to help each other get what they have needed.

1. ☑ **Reading Check** **Tell** how you and your friends help each other.

American Indians Today

Today, many American Indians live throughout the United States. They bring their culture to others. You may see their art, jewelry, or even foods. They also share their stories. They continue to shape our communities.

2. ☑ Reading Check **Look** at the pictures of American Indians from long ago. How do American Indians share their culture today? **Tell** a partner.

Quest Connection

Tell the title of your favorite story.

INTERACTIVITY

Explore stories from different cultures.

Academic Vocabulary

practice • carry out or do

Arts

Some American Indians make jewelry that is worn in celebrations. They **practice** this art form to celebrate their culture. They also make jewelry to sell to other people.

Storytelling is very important in American Indian cultures. Many stories talk about how the world began. Other stories tell about nature.

These stories are called creation stories. Older people pass them down to younger generations. They are **oral** stories, which means they are spoken or sung aloud.

Some oral stories are called **folk tales**.
Folk tales are stories that include myths,
legends, tall tales, fairy tales, and fables.

3. ☑Reading Check **Underline** what many
of the stories are about.

☑Lesson 4 Check

👆 **INTERACTIVITY**

Check your understanding
of the key ideas of this
lesson.

4. **Compare and Contrast Tell** how storytelling
in your culture is similar to or different from
American Indian cultures.

5. **Sequence Look** at the pictures. **Circle** which
came first.

6. **Understand the** *Quest* Connections **What is your**
favorite folk tale? **Share** with a partner.

Artifact: Basket

Some American Indians are skilled basket weavers. This basket was made from reeds. Reeds are a type of plant.

Many American Indians make other tools they use every day, too. They make arrows, knives, and fishing rods out of wood, stone, and plant parts.

This basket tells us more information about American Indian culture. Many people today buy baskets like this to use or to show as artwork.

Primary Source

Using a Primary Source

Write answers to these questions.

1. What was the basket made from?

_____

_____

2. What might have the basket been used for?

_____

_____

3. What does this basket tell us about the people who made it?

_____

_____

_____

Wrap It Up

The American Indians make baskets to carry things. **Think** of an object in your life that you use in a similar way. **Write** about it.

_____

_____

Unlock The BIG Question

I will know how immigrants help define America.

INTERACTIVITY

Participate in a class discussion to preview the content of this lesson.

Vocabulary

immigrant
settled
economy

Academic Vocabulary

contribute

JumpStart Activity

Look at a classroom world map. Talk to a partner about what you see. Say how you could travel to different countries.

Who Is an Immigrant?

An **immigrant** is a person who goes to a new country to live. Immigrants want a good job and a good life for their families.

Many immigrants traveled to the United States on ships. They entered the country through Ellis Island. This is in New York Harbor near the Statue of Liberty.

Other immigrants came through Angel Island. This is in California. Many of these immigrants arrived from Asia. Others came from Mexico and New Zealand.

Once in Ellis Island and Angel Island, immigrants were processed, or checked. Doctors made sure they were not sick or that they would not make others sick. Officers asked questions about their history. Once they passed all the tests, they could enter the country.

1. ☑Reading Check **Compare and Contrast**
Tell how Ellis Island and Angel Island are alike.

Immigrants Helped Our Country

Many early immigrants **settled**, or stayed, in New York and California. Others moved to nearby cities and states.

Once they were settled, they looked for work. They worked hard.
They earned money and spent money.
They helped grow America's **economy**.

2. ✓ **Reading Check** **Circle** how immigrants helped our country.

Immigrants Today

Immigrants from around the world continue to settle in our country.

They bring their music, food, stories, and traditions to their new communities. They work hard and **contribute** to the economy. Immigrants continue to shape our culture.

Academic Vocabulary

contribute • add to; help

INTERACTIVITY

Check your understanding of the key ideas of this lesson.

☑ Lesson 5 Check

3. **Main Idea and Details Finish** the sentence. Many immigrants came to the United States through

   _____

   _____.

4. **Finish** the sentence. Immigrants bring their

   _____

   _____

   _____ to our country.

5. **Think** about your city or town. **Tell** a partner how immigrants make your city or town a more interesting place.

6 Stories in Our Culture

Unlock The BIG Question

I will know about what stories can teach us.

🖱 INTERACTIVITY

Participate in a class discussion to preview the content of this lesson.

Vocabulary

legends
morals
clever

JumpStart Activity

As a group, create a skit about a story you know. Act it out!

Folk Tales and Legends

Folk tales and **legends** are traditional stories that are passed down through time. They can be about almost anything. The Chinese folk tale "The Four Dragons" is a tale about how rivers began. Other folk tales may be about why traditions happen or what people do in their ceremonies.

1. ☑**Reading Check** **Tell** if you think your favorite folk tale is true or not.

Life Lessons

Most cultures have their own folk tales and legends. Many of these stories are similar, though. They teach people lessons about life.

These life lessons are called **morals**. Some morals teach good behaviors and how people can be nicer to each other. Other morals teach how to make your life better.

2. ☑ **Reading Check** **Draw** a character in your favorite folk tale. **Tell** about the moral of the story. How it is similar or different from another folk tale you know?

"The Tiger and the Frog"

first

next

then

finally

"The Tiger and the Frog" is a Hmong folk tale. In the story, Tiger and Frog decide to race to the top of a mountain.

Frog is worried because Tiger is very fast. Frog stops and asks his frog friends for help. The frogs hide in different places up the mountain. They all pretend to be Frog.

Tiger runs fast up the mountain. On the way, he calls out to Frog. Each time, a different frog answers. Tiger runs faster. Soon he is too tired to continue. Frog wins the race!

This story teaches a lesson. Be **clever**, or very smart, and you can win any race!

3. ☑ **Reading Check** Sequence **Retell** the story to a partner. **Say** what happens first, next, then, and finally.

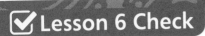
☑ **Lesson 6 Check**

4. **Ask and Answer Questions Check** the two correct answers.

   Folk tales and legends …

   [ ] are always true.

   [ ] are passed down.

   [ ] are usually told aloud.

5. **Sequence Think** about the story of "The Tiger and the Frog." What do you think might happen after the race? **Draw** a picture.

6. **Compare** the story of "The Tiger and the Frog" to a story in your culture. **Tell** what is similar and what is different.

Sequence

Sequence is the order in which things happen. We use clue words to help us figure out order. Some clue words are *first*, *next*, *then*, and *finally*.

Look at the pictures and read the sentences. See how the sentences match the order of the pictures.

"The Cherokee Legend of Why Rabbit Has a Short Tail"

First, Rabbit showed off his very long tail to Fox.

Next, Fox tied a fish to his tail. He wanted Rabbit to think there were fish in the water.

Then, Rabbit put his long tail in the water to try to catch fish.

Finally, the water froze on Rabbit's tail. Now his tail is short.

🖱 **INTERACTIVITY**

Review and practice what you learned about sequence.

1. We can use sequence words to tell about real events, too. **Read** about Mr. Kim's day. **Look** at the pictures. **Underline** the clue word for each step of what Mr. Kim does.

Mr. Kim is going to work today. First, he gets dressed. Next, he walks to the train station. Then, Mr. Kim arrives at his office. Finally, he sits down at his desk and gets to work.

Quality:
Patriotism

Irving Berlin
Immigrant and Patriot

Songwriter Irving Berlin was a Jewish immigrant. He came to the United States with his family from Russia in 1893. They lived in New York.

Berlin is known as one of America's greatest songwriters. One of his most famous songs is "God Bless America." This patriotic song is still sung today. Berlin also wrote many other patriotic songs.

Write what makes you think that Berlin loved his country.

_____

_____

_____

Talk About It
Tell how you can show your patriotism.

☑ Assessment

 GAMES

Play the vocabulary game.

Vocabulary and Key Ideas

1. Fill in the correct circle.

A tradition …

Ⓐ happens one time only.

Ⓑ happens many times.

Ⓒ has not happened yet.

2. Sequence Write the word that comes last. _____

first, next, then, _____

3. Look at the pictures. **Look** at the timeline. **Draw** a line from the number on the timeline to the correct picture.

| 1 | 2 | 3 |

4. Check each correct answer:
American Indians made . . .

A. [ ] tools

B. [ ] baskets

C. [ ] jewelry

Critical Thinking and Writing

5. Draw a traditional object from your culture. **Compare** it to one you learned about in the lesson.

Quest Findings

INTERACTIVITY

Use this activity to help you prepare to make your flag.

Make Your Culture Flag

It's time to help Annie make a culture flag. Then show and tell!

1 Prepare to Draw

Work in a small group. Think about your traditions and celebrations. *What foods do you eat? What do you wear? What languages do you speak?*

2 Create Your Culture Flag

Draw symbols that show the diverse cultures in our state. Show how we are all different. Put all your symbols together onto one flag. Make sure to include different cultures.

3 Write About Your Flag

Ask and answer questions about the symbols on your flag. Write about what each symbol stands for.

4 Show and Tell

Share your flag with the class, and celebrate our diverse state!

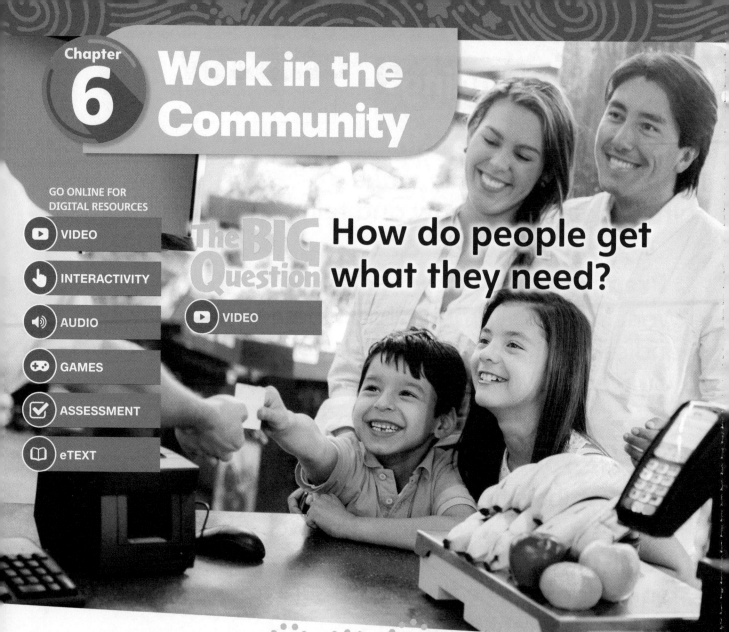

Work in the Community

GO ONLINE FOR
DIGITAL RESOURCES

▶ VIDEO

👆 INTERACTIVITY

🔊 AUDIO

🎮 GAMES

☑ ASSESSMENT

📖 eTEXT

The BIG Question

How do people get what they need?

▶ VIDEO

Jumpstart Activity

👆 INTERACTIVITY

Act out a scene in a store. Take turns acting as workers and shoppers.

AUDIO

Needs and Wants

Preview the chapter **vocabulary** by singing the song to the tune of "Are You Sleeping?"

Consumers have needs,
producers give them choices.
Needs and wants.
Needs and wants.

Jobs provide us money,
to spend on goods and services.
Work, save, spend.
Work, save, spend.

Quest

Writing Using Sources

Help Stan Make a Money Plan

Quest Kick Off

I'm Stan. I love numbers! I just won $10 in a math contest. Can you help me plan how to spend my prize money?

👆 **INTERACTIVITY**

Explore some things Stan could do.

1 Start with a Brainstorm

Think about what you might do with the money. Would you save it or spend it? What would you buy? Write your ideas.

2 Look for *Quest* Connections

Turn to the next page to begin looking for Quest Connections. They will help you make a plan.

3 Write Up Your *Quest* Findings

Use the Quest Findings page at the end of the chapter to help you write your plan.

Needs, Wants, and Choices

I will know how to choose between needs and wants.

INTERACTIVITY

Participate in a class discussion to preview the content of this lesson.

Vocabulary

needs

wants

choice

Academic Vocabulary

limited

JumpStart Activity

Take turns with a partner and act out something you would like to have. Guess what it is.

People Have Needs

Things people must have to live are called **needs**. Food, water, clothes, and a place to live are needs. Some people grow their own food. Other people buy food.

1. ☑ **Reading Check** Main Idea and Details **Circle** the needs in the picture.

People Have Wants

Things people would like to have are called **wants**. A toy is a want. It is fun to play with. But a person does not need toys to live.

2. ☑**Reading Check** **Look** at the chart. **Write** one more need and one more want.

Needs	Wants
Home	Bike
Clothes	TV

Quest Connections

Think about how you would choose between two wants.

INTERACTIVITY

Learn more about how to choose between wants.

Making Choices

We cannot have all the things we want and need. We must make choices. A **choice** is when we pick, or choose, between two or more things.

Most people use money to buy needs and wants. The money we have is usually **limited**.

Academic Vocabulary

limited • having only a set amount

Before we buy wants, we must meet all our needs. If there is money left over, we can spend it on wants.

Word Wise

Multiple Meanings

Meet can mean *get together*. What do you think "meet a need" means?

3. ☑ **Reading Check** **Highlight words that tell how to make choices.**

☑ **Lesson 1 Check**

● **INTERACTIVITY**

Check your understanding of the key ideas of this lesson.

4. **Sequence** What should you do before you buy something you want?

_____

_____

_____

5. How can people meet their needs?

_____

_____

_____

6. **Understand the** *Quest* **Connection** **Talk** with a partner. **Tell** about a time you made a choice.

Lesson 2 Goods and Services

Unlock The BIG Question

I will know what goods and services are.

INTERACTIVITY

Participate in a class discussion to preview the content of this lesson.

Vocabulary

goods
services

JumpStart Activity

Tell a partner what you use to help make your favorite meal.

Goods at Home

Goods are things that people grow or make. Most people today buy goods from others. Some of the goods people use at home are food, dishes, tables, and chairs.

1. ☑ **Reading Check** **Draw** a picture of a good you use at home.

Goods in School and the Community

You use goods at school. Your school has books and computers. You use goods in your community. You may choose to buy a toy.

2. ☑ **Reading Check** **On the line, write the name of another kind of good used in school.**

I use _____ at school.

Quest Connection
Underline a good and a service.

🖑 **INTERACTIVITY**
Learn more about goods and services.

a city bus driver

School and Community Services

Services are tasks that people do to help others. You can see many service workers at school. Your teacher helps you learn. A cook makes you lunch.

There are many services in the community. Some service workers are firefighters, nurses, store clerks, and bus drivers.

3. ☑ **Reading Check** Main Idea and Details **Write** one thing a service worker does.

_____

_____

_____

_____

4. Main Idea and Details Name a service at school. Why is it important?

_____

_____

_____

_____

_____

5. What kind of service would you like to do for other people?

_____

_____

_____

_____

_____

6. Understand the *Quest* **Connection** What is a good or service you might want to buy?

_____

_____

_____

_____

_____

Identify Main Idea and Details

The most important idea in a text is the main idea. It is often found in the first sentence of a paragraph. Other sentences give details. They support or tell more about the main idea.

main idea > Sofia and her parents shop for her class picnic. They are buying vegetables.

details > Sofia chooses beans.

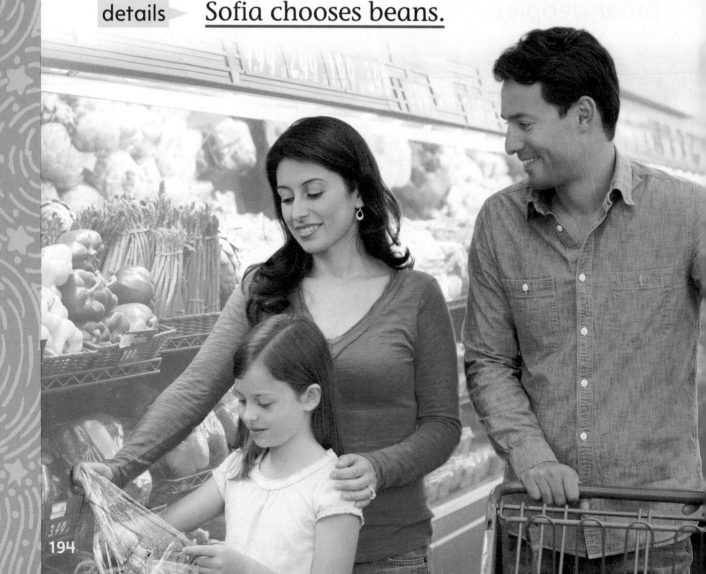

Your Turn!

1. Read the paragraph. **Circle** the main idea. **Underline** a sentence that gives a detail.

 INTERACTIVITY

Review and practice what you learned about how to identify a main idea and details.

Our class visited the school library. We learned how to find books about animals. The librarian showed us how to take out a book. My friend Cho got a book about lions.

2. Write a sentence that tells how the details support the main idea.

_____

_____

_____

_____

_____

3 Producers and Consumers

I will know who producers and consumers are.

👆 **INTERACTIVITY**

Participate in a class discussion to preview the content of this lesson.

Vocabulary

producer
consumer
market

Academic Vocabulary

order

JumpStart Activity

Share with a partner a good you would like to make to sell.

Who Are Producers?

A **producer** provides goods or services. Farmers and carpenters produce goods. Doctors provide services.

1. ☑ **Reading Check** Main Idea and Details **Circle** the producer in the picture.

Who Are Consumers?

A **consumer** buys or uses goods and services. Some goods come from nearby. Others come from far away.

Producers can be consumers, too. They buy goods they need. A carpenter needs wood, glue, and nails to make a chair.

2. ☑**Reading Check** Main Idea and Details **Draw** an X on the good in the picture.

Buying and Selling

Producers **market**, or sell, their goods and services. They can sell goods and services to a store. Some producers sell goods online. Consumers **order** from their computers.

Some goods come from far away. Wood for a house may come from other states or countries.

3. ☑Reading Check In the picture, **circle** a producer. **Draw** an X on a consumer.

Academic Vocabulary

order • to ask a company to send to you a good you buy

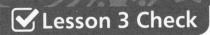
Lesson 3 Check

4. Main Idea and Details How can a person be both a producer and a consumer?

5. Highlight how producers earn money with their goods and services.

6. Would you choose to buy goods made in your own community or from far away? Why?

We Spend, Budget, and Save

Unlock
The **BIG**
Question

I will know how people spend and save money.

INTERACTIVITY

Participate in a class discussion to preview the content of this lesson.

Vocabulary

spend
budget
donate
save

JumPstart Activity

Make up a story about the people in the picture. Share it with a partner.

Spending Money

Long ago, people exchanged, or traded, goods and services. A farmer could trade food for a doctor's help. Today, most families **spend**, or use, money. They buy goods and services. But money is limited.

Making a Budget

Many families make a **budget**. A budget is a plan for how to spend money. Budgets list needs before wants. Some families also **donate**, or give money to others.

1. ☑**Reading Check** Main Idea and Details **Write** one more want in the family's budget chart.

Budget Money to Spend: $100	
Needs:	
Food	$25
Clothing	$15
Home	$45
Wants:	
New game	$10
	$5

Saving Money

Quest Connection

Think about Stan's money. How would you divide the money to spend, save, and donate?

INTERACTIVITY

Learn how to divide Stan's money.

Some wants cost a lot of money. A new computer is an example of a want. A family may have to **save**, or keep, money. They save until they can buy the computer.

2. ☑ Reading Check **Highlight what a family might need to save money to buy.**

☑ Lesson 4 Check

3. Summarize What is a budget?

_____

_____

_____

_____

_____

4. Why do families save money?

_____

_____

_____

_____

_____

5. Understand the Quest Connection Identify the different ways to use the prize money.

_____

_____

_____

Analyze Costs and Benefits

When you spend money, you must make choices. Every choice has a cost. The cost is what you give up when you make a choice. The benefit is what you get in return.

You may have to choose between two toys. The benefit is the toy you chose. One cost is the money you paid for that toy. Another cost is the toy that you did not choose. When you chose not to buy that toy, you gave it up.

Your Turn!

Jen has saved enough money
to buy a basketball or a game.
Look at the chart.

INTERACTIVITY

Review and practice
what you learned about
costs and benefits.

1. What would you choose? **Mark** an X in a box
to show your choice.

Jen's Choices				
Activity	Benefits	Cost (What you pay)	Cost (What you give up)	Choice
Game 	1. Play inside or outside 2. Play with others	$15	the basketball	☐
Basketball	1. Play outside 2. Play with others or alone	$20		☐

2. What does Jen give up if she chooses the basketball?
Write the answer on the line in the chart.

Unlock The BIG Question

I will know that people work at jobs.

INTERACTIVITY

Participate in a class discussion to preview the content of this lesson.

Vocabulary

job
work

Academic Vocabulary

develop

JumpStart Activity

Work with a partner to act out some things you do to help your parents at home.

Jobs at Home

A **job** is what people do to produce goods or services. Jobs take special skills. Sewing clothes is a skill. **Work** is what a person does at a job.

Workers do jobs in the home. Some people who work at home earn money. Others choose to work in the home without pay. They care for their families.

Jobs in the Community

People have many kinds of jobs in the community. Jobs often focus on one special task. Workers learn how to use tools to build houses. Other workers learn how to sell houses to families.

We can buy goods from all over the world. Some workers drive trucks and trains to move goods. Airplane pilots move goods, too. They land at airports around the world. They pick up and deliver goods at the airport.

1. ☑**Reading Check** Main Idea and Details **Highlight** the main idea of the first paragraph. **Circle** two details.

Jobs at School

Academic Vocabulary

develop • to make better

Many people work in your school. Teachers help you learn. Cooks feed you at lunchtime. Coaches help you **develop** skills in sports.

You have a job to do at school, too. You must work hard to learn. You should listen, ask questions, and do your best.

2. ☑ Reading Check **Work** with a partner. **Talk** about how schools today are different than the school in the picture.

INTERACTIVITY

Check your understanding of the key ideas of this lesson.

3. Main Idea and Details What is a job?

_____

_____

_____

_____

_____

4. Why do some people do jobs that do not earn money?

_____

_____

_____

_____

5. What job would you like to do? What would you need to know to do the job?

_____

_____

_____

_____

_____

Photograph: Loading Trucks

Many producers send goods to consumers who are far away. How do workers move all the goods from one place to another?

This photograph is a primary source. It shows how goods are moved on trucks. Look carefully at the photograph. Think about what you see.

Primary Source

Using a Primary Source

Look at the photograph to answer these questions.

1. What is the worker doing?

_____

_____

_____

_____

2. Circle a tool the worker uses to load the truck.

Wrap It Up

Fill in the blank with a skill that this worker must have.

A worker who loads trucks must know how to

_____

_____

_____

_____

**Quality:
Individual
responsibility**

Sophie Cubbison
Health Food Pioneer

Sophie Cubbison was born in 1890. She grew up on a ranch in San Marcos, California. By the time she was 16 years old, Sophie cooked meals for more than 40 ranch workers. The workers ate breakfast at 5:00 A.M. Dinner was at 8:30 P.M. Cooking was a big responsibility.

As an adult, Sophie opened her own bakery business. She made recipes for healthy foods.

How were Sophie's responsibilities at work like those of people today?

☑ **Assessment**

🎮 GAME

Play the vocabulary game.

Vocabulary and Key Ideas

1. Fill in the circle next to the best answer. What are **services**?

(A) things that people grow or make

(B) jobs that people do to help others

(C) plans for spending money

(D) things you must have to live

2. Write each word in the correct row.

clothing	toys	food
games	home	bike

Needs			
Wants			

3. Draw a line. **Match** each word to a picture.

Producer   Consumer

Critical Thinking and Writing

4. Look at the chart. **Decide** which activity to do. **Mark** an X for your choice.

Activity	Benefits	Cost (What you pay)	Cost (What you give up)	Choice
Movie	1. Happens once 2. See with friends and family	$5	Game	☐
Game	1. Play more than once 2. Play with friends	$15	Movie	☐

5. Write the reason you made that choice.

_____

_____

_____

_____

Quest Findings

Use this activity to help you prepare to make Stan's money plan.

Write Your Plan

It's time to write your plan for how Stan can spend his prize money.

1 Make a Choice
How did you decide to spend the money? Write about your choice.

2 Use a Chart
Fill out a chart like this one to show your plan.

3 Think About Choices
Write about why you made the choices you did.

4 Share Your Choices
Share your chart with the class.

Questions	My Plan
Will you buy needs or wants?	
Will you buy goods or services?	
How much will you spend?	
How much will you save?	
How much will you donate?	

The United States of America, Political

Washington
★Olympia

★Salem

Oregon

Montana
★Helena

North Dakota
★Bismarck

★Boise
Idaho

South Dakota
Pierre★

Wyoming

Salt Lake City ★

Cheyenne ★

Sacramento ★

Carson City ★

Nevada

Utah

Denver ★

Colorado

Nebraska

Lincoln★

Topeka ★

Kansas

California

Arizona
★Phoenix

Santa Fe ★

New Mexico

Oklahoma

Oklahoma ★ City

PACIFIC OCEAN

Texas

★Austin

Alaska

MEXICO

★Honolulu

Juneau★

Hawaii

CANADA

Minnesota

St. Paul

Michigan

Wisconsin

Madison
Lansing

Iowa

Des Moines

Indiana

Indianapolis

Springfield

Illinois

Jefferson
City

Missouri

Ohio
Columbus

New Hampshire

Vermont

Montpelier

Albany

New York

Hartford

Pennsylvania

Harrisburg

Annapolis

Maine

Augusta

Concord

Massachusetts

Boston

Providence

Rhode Island

Connecticut

Trenton   New Jersey

Dover

Delaware

Maryland

Washington, D.C.

Virginia

West
Virginia

Charleston

Frankfort

Richmond

Kentucky

Arkansas

Little
Rock

Mississippi

Louisiana

Baton
Rouge

Nashville

Tennessee

Alabama   Atlanta

Montgomery

Jackson

Georgia

Tallahassee

Florida

Raleigh   North
Carolina

Columbia

South
Carolina

ATLANTIC
OCEAN

Gulf of Mexico

N
W   E
S

Legend

⊛ National
capital

★ State
capital

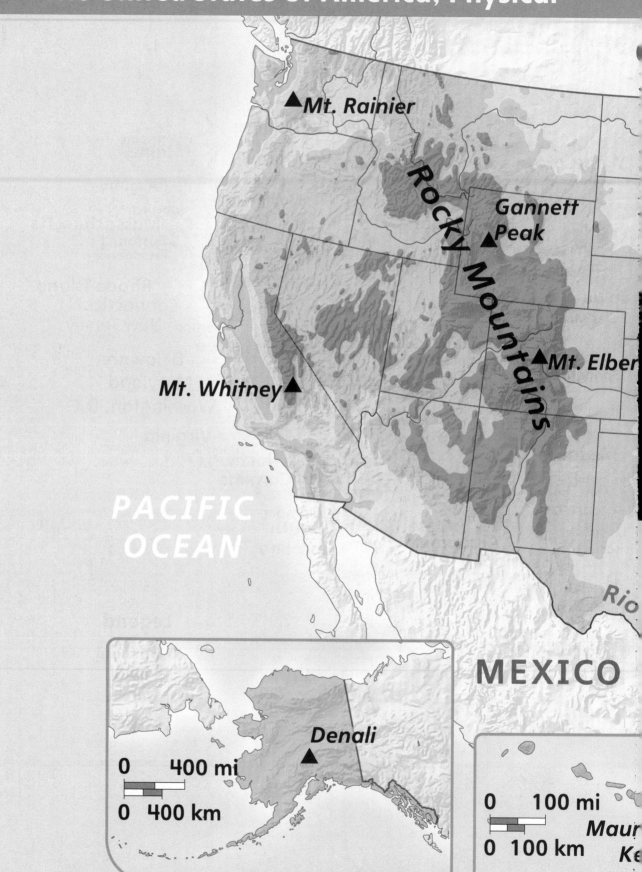

Mt. Rainier

Rocky Mountains

Gannett Peak

Mt. Elber

Mt. Whitney

PACIFIC OCEAN

Rio

MEXICO

Denali

0   400 mi

0   400 km

0   100 mi

Maur

0   100 km   Ke

CANADA

0 ——— 400 mi

0 ——— 400 km

Great Lakes

Great Plains

Appalachian Mts.

ATLANTIC OCEAN

Gulf of Mexico

Grande

Legend
Elevation

Feet		Meters
10,000		3,048
6,000		1,829
3,000		914
1,000		305
500		152
0		0

▲ Peak

R3

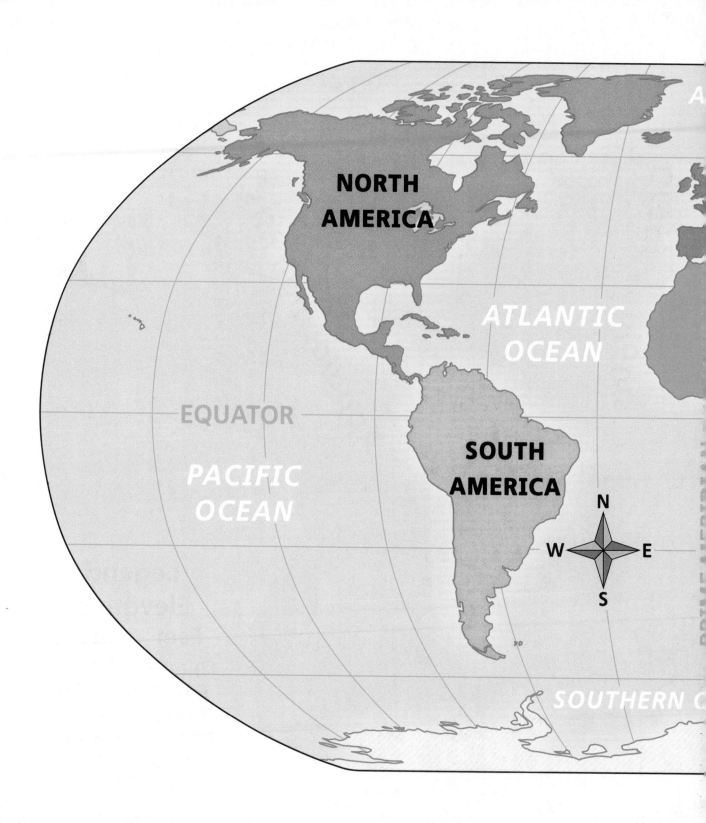

NORTH AMERICA

ATLANTIC OCEAN

EQUATOR

SOUTH AMERICA

PACIFIC OCEAN

N
W E
S

SOUTHERN O

compass rose A tool that shows the cardinal directions. NOUN

consequence What happens when we do not follow rules or laws. NOUN

conservation The protection of our land, water, and plants. NOUN

constitution A written set of laws. NOUN

consume To use up. VERB

consumer Someone who buys or uses goods and services. NOUN

continent A large area of land. NOUN

contribute To add to; help. VERB

cooperate To work together. VERB

country A nation. NOUN

create To make something. VERB

culture The way a group of people live. NOUN

custom Something that a person usually does in a certain way. NOUN

D

debate To talk about something. VERB

decade A ten year period. NOUN

democracy A government where its citizens make decisions or where leaders are chosen to make the decisions. NOUN

demonstrations Public meetings or marches against something that is not right. NOUN

describe To tell about something. VERB

develop To make better. VERB

direction A statement that tells which way to go or where something is. NOUN

diverse Come from different countries or have different backgrounds and experiences. ADJECTIVE

document A piece of paper with important information. NOUN

donate To give money to others. VERB

E

economy The system of earning and using money. NOUN

emblem A symbol. NOUN

environment The air, weather, land, water, and living things in a place. NOUN

F

festival A special time. NOUN

flag A piece of cloth with colors and patterns. NOUN

folk tale An oral story that includes myths, legends, tall tales, fairy tales, and fables. NOUN

freedom The ability to do as one wants. NOUN

future What will happen later. NOUN

G

general Broad or basic. ADJECTIVE

generation People who were born at about the same time. NOUN

globe A model of Earth. NOUN

goal Something you hope to do or get. NOUN

goods Things that people grow or make. NOUN

government A group of citizens who makes laws and makes sure we follow them. NOUN

governor The leader of a state. NOUN

grand Important. ADJECTIVE

graph A diagram that shows information. NOUN

guardian A leader who takes care of us at home. NOUN

H

hero Someone who works hard to help others. NOUN

history The story of the past. NOUN

I

immigrant A person who goes to a new country to live. NOUN

invention Something that is made for the first time. NOUN

J

job What people do to produce goods or services. NOUN

justice Fair treatment. NOUN

L

landmark A famous thing that is well known. NOUN

law A community rule. NOUN

leader A person who helps people decide what to do and how to do it. NOUN

legend A key that tells what the symbols on a map mean. NOUN

legend A traditional story that is passed down through time. NOUN

limited Having only a set amount. ADJECTIVE

location Where something is. NOUN

M

manners The ways we are polite. NOUN

map A drawing of a place. NOUN

map legend A box that shows what the symbols mean on a map. NOUN

map scale A line on a map that shows the distance in the real world. NOUN

market To sell. VERB

mayor A leader of a community government. NOUN

measure To find out the size or amount of something. VERB

memorial Something people build to honor a person or event. NOUN

migrant worker A person who moves from place to place for work. NOUN

military Having to do with soldiers. NOUN

model A three-dimensional version of something, but much smaller. NOUN

moral A life lesson. NOUN

N

national Something belonging to a nation. ADJECTIVE

needs Things people must have to live. NOUN

O

ocean A large body of salty water. NOUN

oral Spoken or sung aloud. ADJECTIVE

order To ask a company to send to you a good you buy. VERB

P

past What happened before. NOUN

plains Flat lands with few trees. NOUN

pledge A promise. NOUN

practice To carry out or do. VERB

present Today. NOUN

president The leader of a country. NOUN

primary source A source made by a person who was at an event. NOUN

producer Someone who provides goods or services. NOUN

R

relative location Where something is as compared to something else. NOUN

responsibility Something we do because we have to or because it is the right thing. NOUN

right Something we are free to do or have. NOUN

rule A statement that tells us what to do and what not to do. NOUN

S

save To keep money. VERB

secondary source A source made after an event happened. NOUN

service A task that people do to help others. NOUN

settle To stay. VERB

solve To fix a problem. VERB

spend To use money. VERB

storytelling Sharing stories with a group. NOUN

succeed To do well. VERB

symbol A picture that stands for a real thing. NOUN

symbolize To stand for. VERB

 T

tally A mark. NOUN

technology The use of science to solve problems. NOUN

town A small community. NOUN

trade To exchange. VERB

tradition Something passed down over time. NOUN

transportation The way people move from place to place. NOUN

 V

veteran A man or woman who served in the armed forces. NOUN

vote To make a choice that gets counted. VERB

 W

wants Things people would like to have. NOUN

weather What it is like outside. NOUN

work What a person does at a job. VERB

Glosario

A

absolute location/ubicación absoluta El punto exacto donde está un lugar. SUSTANTIVO

amendment/enmienda Cambio. SUSTANTIVO

anthem/himno Canción de elogio. SUSTANTIVO

armed forces/fuerzas armadas Todos los soldados que protegen un país. SUSTANTIVO

artifact/artefacto Objeto hecho por personas. SUSTANTIVO

B

ballot/boleta electoral Hoja de papel usada para que un voto sea secreto. SUSTANTIVO

belief/creencia Algo que una persona piensa que es cierto. SUSTANTIVO

benefit/beneficiarse Obtener algo a cambio. VERBO

biography/biografía Libro acerca de la vida de una persona. SUSTANTIVO

brainstorm/hacer una lluvia de ideas Crear muchas ideas. VERBO

budget/presupuesto Plan para saber cómo gastar dinero. SUSTANTIVO

C

calendar/calendario Muestra los días, las semanas y los meses del año. SUSTANTIVO

cardinal directions/puntos cardinales Norte, sur, este y oeste. SUSTANTIVO

cause/causa La razón de que algo ocurra. SUSTANTIVO

century/siglo Período de 100 años. SUSTANTIVO

ceremony/ceremonia Un evento especial e importante. SUSTANTIVO

choice/elección La acción de elegir entre dos o más cosas. SUSTANTIVO

citizen/ciudadano Persona que pertenece a un estado o país. SUSTANTIVO

city/ciudad Comunidad grande con muchas personas. SUSTANTIVO

clever/listo Inteligente. ADJETIVO

colony/colonia Territorio controlado por otro país. SUSTANTIVO

communicate/comunicarse Compartir información con otros. VERBO

community/comunidad Lugar donde las personas y las familias viven, trabajan y se divierten. SUSTANTIVO

compass rose/rosa de los vientos Instrumento que muestra los puntos cardinales. SUSTANTIVO

consequence/consecuencia Lo que ocurre cuando uno no sigue las reglas o leyes. SUSTANTIVO

conservation/conservación La protección de nuestra tierra, agua y plantas. SUSTANTIVO

constitution/constitución Un conjunto de leyes escritas. SUSTANTIVO

consume/consumir Agotar. VERBO

consumer/consumidor Alguien que compra o usa bienes y servicios. SUSTANTIVO

continent/continente Gran área de tierra. SUSTANTIVO

contribute/contribuir Colaborar; ayudar. VERBO

cooperate/cooperar Trabajar en conjunto. VERBO

country/país Una nación. SUSTANTIVO

create/crear Hacer algo. VERBO

culture/cultura La forma de vida de un grupo de personas. SUSTANTIVO

custom/costumbre Algo que una persona suele hacer de cierta manera. SUSTANTIVO

D

debate/debatir Hablar acerca de algo. VERBO

decade/década Período de 10 años. SUSTANTIVO

democracy/democracia Gobierno donde los ciudadanos toman las decisiones o donde los líderes son elegidos para tomar las decisiones. SUSTANTIVO

demonstrations/manifestaciones
Reuniones públicas o marchas contra algo que no está bien. SUSTANTIVO

describe/describir Explicar cómo es algo. VERBO

develop/desarrollar Mejorar. VERBO

direction/dirección Enunciado que dice hacia dónde ir o dónde está algo. SUSTANTIVO

diverse/diverso Que viene de diferentes países o tiene diferente origen y experiencias. ADJETIVO

document/documento Hoja de papel con información importante. SUSTANTIVO

donate/donar Dar dinero a otras personas. VERBO

E

economy/economía El sistema de ganar y usar dinero. SUSTANTIVO

emblem/emblema Símbolo. SUSTANTIVO

environment/medio ambiente El aire, el clima, la tierra, el agua y los seres vivientes de un lugar. SUSTANTIVO

F

festival/festival Una ocasión especial. SUSTANTIVO

flag/bandera Un trozo de tela con colores y dibujos. SUSTANTIVO

folk tale/cuento folklórico Cuento oral que incluye mitos, leyendas, cuentos exagerados, cuentos de hadas y fábulas. SUSTANTIVO

freedom/libertad La posibilidad de hacer lo que uno quiere. SUSTANTIVO

future/futuro Lo que ocurrirá más adelante. SUSTANTIVO

G

general/general Amplio o básico. ADJETIVO

generation/generación Personas que nacieron y viven aproximadamente al mismo tiempo. SUSTANTIVO

globe/globo terráqueo Un modelo de la Tierra. SUSTANTIVO

goal/meta Algo que uno espera hacer o conseguir. SUSTANTIVO

goods/bienes Algo que las personas cultivan o hacen. SUSTANTIVO

government/gobierno Grupo de ciudadanos que elaboran leyes y se aseguran de que las sigamos. SUSTANTIVO

governor/gobernador El líder de un estado. SUSTANTIVO

grand/grandioso Importante. ADJETIVO

graph/gráfica Diagrama que muestra información. SUSTANTIVO

guardian/tutor Líder que nos cuida en nuestra casa. SUSTANTIVO

hero/héroe Alguien que trabaja duro para ayudar a otros. SUSTANTIVO

history/historia El relato de lo que ocurrió en el pasado. SUSTANTIVO

immigrant/inmigrante Persona que se va a vivir a otro país. SUSTANTIVO

invention/invento Algo hecho por primera vez. SUSTANTIVO

job/trabajo Lo que hacen las personas para producir bienes o servicios. SUSTANTIVO

justice/justicia Trato justo. SUSTANTIVO

landmark/sitio de interés Algo que es famoso y bien conocido. SUSTANTIVO

law/ley Una regla de la comunidad. SUSTANTIVO

leader/líder Persona que ayuda a la gente a decidir qué hacer y cómo hacerlo. SUSTANTIVO

legend/leyenda Clave que indica lo que significan los símbolos de un mapa. SUSTANTIVO

legend/leyenda Cuento tradicional que se transmite a lo largo del tiempo. SUSTANTIVO

limited/limitado Que tiene solo una cantidad fija. ADJETIVO

location/ubicación Dónde está algo. SUSTANTIVO

M

manners/modales La manera en que somos respetuosos. SUSTANTIVO

map/mapa Dibujo de un lugar. SUSTANTIVO

map legend/leyenda de un mapa Caja que muestra lo que significan los símbolos de un mapa. SUSTANTIVO

map scale/escala de un mapa Línea en un mapa que muestra la distancia en el mundo real. SUSTANTIVO

market/comercializar Vender. VERBO

mayor/alcalde Líder del gobierno de una comunidad. SUSTANTIVO

measure/medir Averiguar el tamaño o la cantidad de algo. VERBO

memorial/monumento Algo construido por la gente para honrar a una persona o un suceso. SUSTANTIVO

migrant worker/trabajador migratorio Persona que se muda de un lugar a otro por trabajo. SUSTANTIVO

military/militar Relacionado con soldados. SUSTANTIVO

model/modelo Versión tridimensional de algo, pero de un tamaño mucho más pequeño. SUSTANTIVO

moral/moraleja Lección de vida. SUSTANTIVO

motto/lema Una expresión. SUSTANTIVO

N

national/nacional Algo que pertenece a la nación. ADJETIVO

needs/necesidades Cosas que las personas deben tener para vivir. SUSTANTIVO

O

ocean/océano Gran masa de agua salada. SUSTANTIVO

oral/oral Hablado o cantado en voz alta. ADJETIVO

order/encargar Pedir a una empresa que te envíe un bien que vas a comprar. VERBO

P

past/pasado Lo que ocurrió antes. SUSTANTIVO

plains/llanura Tierra plana con pocos árboles. SUSTANTIVO

pledge/juramento Promesa. SUSTANTIVO

practice/practicar Llevar a cabo o hacer. VERBO

present/presente Hoy. SUSTANTIVO

president/presidente El líder de un país. SUSTANTIVO

primary source/fuente primaria Fuente hecha por una persona que estuvo cuando ocurrió un suceso. SUSTANTIVO

producer/productor Alguien que da bienes o servicios. SUSTANTIVO

R

relative location/ubicación relativa Dónde está algo en comparación con otra cosa. SUSTANTIVO

responsibility/responsabilidad Lo que hacemos porque debemos o porque es lo correcto. SUSTANTIVO

right/derecho Algo que somos libres de hacer o tener. SUSTANTIVO

rule/regla Algo que nos dice qué hacer y qué no hacer. SUSTANTIVO

S

save/ahorrar Guardar dinero. VERBO

secondary source/fuente secundaria Fuente hecha después de que ocurrió un suceso. SUSTANTIVO

service/servicio Tarea que hacen las personas para ayudar a otros. SUSTANTIVO

settle/establecerse Quedarse. VERBO

solve/solucionar Resolver un problema. VERBO

spend/gastar Usar dinero. VERBO

storytelling/narración La acción de compartir cuentos con un grupo. SUSTANTIVO

succeed/tener éxito Hacer algo con buenos resultados. VERBO

symbol/símbolo Una imagen que representa algo real. SUSTANTIVO

symbolize/simbolizar Representar. VERBO

T

tally/marca de conteo Una marca que ayuda a contar. SUSTANTIVO

technology/tecnología El uso de la ciencia para resolver problemas. SUSTANTIVO

town/pueblo Comunidad pequeña. SUSTANTIVO

trade/intercambiar Cambiar. VERBO

tradition/tradición Algo que se transmite a otros a lo largo del tiempo. SUSTANTIVO

transportation/medio de transporte La forma en que la gente va de un lugar a otro. SUSTANTIVO

veteran/veterano Hombre o mujer que prestó servicio en las fuerzas armadas. SUSTANTIVO

vote/votar Tomar una decisión que va a ser contada. VERBO

wants/deseos Algo que a la gente le gustaría tener. SUSTANTIVO

weather/estado del tiempo Cómo está el día afuera. SUSTANTIVO

work/trabajar Lo que una persona hace en su empleo. VERBO

Index

This index lists the pages on which topics appear in this book. Page numbers followed by *m* refer to maps. Page numbers followed by *p* refer to photographs. Page numbers followed by *c* refer to charts or graphs. Page numbers followed by *t* refer to timelines. Bold page numbers indicate vocabulary definitions. The terms *See* and *See also* direct the reader to alternate entries.

Credits

Text Acknowledgments

Regents of the University of California

Interview with Sally Paterson Adams conducted by Knox Mellon from The Patterson Family and Ranch: Southern Alameda County In Transition, Vol. III., The Patterson Ranch. Past and Future: The Family's Perspective. Copyright © Regents of the University of California 1988.

Images

Cover

Jim Cummins/The Image Bank/Getty Images;

Front Matter

Copyright Page: Rachid Dahnoun/Aurora Open RF/Alamy Stock Photo; i: Finn Jaschik/Alltravel/Alamy Stock Photo; iii: Camarillo Dr. Albert M.; iii: Dr. James B. Kracht; iii: Dr. Kathy Swan; iii: Dr. Linda B. Bennett; iii: Elfrieda H. Hiebert; iii: Jim Cummins; iii: Kathy Tuchman Glass; iii: Paul Apodaca; iii: Dr. Shirley A. James Hanshaw; iii: Warren J. Blumenfeld; iii: Xiaojian Zhao; xiiiT: Pixelprof/E+/Getty Images; xiv: National Baseball Hall of Fame Library/Major League Baseball Platinum/Getty Images; xiiiB: Everett Historical/Shutterstock; xviii: Espies/Shutterstock; xix: Bettmann/Getty Images; xixBKGD: Fckncg/123RF; SSH1: KidStock/Blend Images/Getty Images; SSH2: Ian Dagnall/Alamy Stock Photo; SSH2: Tom Merton/OJO Images/Getty Images; SSH3B: Photo Researchers, Inc/Alamy Stock Photo; SSH3C: Bachrach/Archive Photos/Getty Images; SSH3T: Dorothea Lange/Library of Congress Prints and Photographs Division[LC-DIG-ppmsca-12883]; SSH4L: Rich Pedroncelli/AP Images; SSH4R: Michael Bush/UPI Photo Service/Newscom; SSH5[a]: Rachid Dahnoun/Alamy Stock Photo; SSH5[b]: Sieboldianus/E+/Getty Images; SSH5[c]: Peter Himmelhuber/Zoonar GmbH/Alamy Stock Photo; SSH5[d]: EmilyKam/iStock/Getty Images; SSH5[e]: Mark Weber/Age Fotostock/Getty Images; SSH5[f]: Robertnowland/iStock/Getty Images; SSH6: Marc Romanelli/Blend Images/Getty Images; SSH7: FatCamera/E+/Getty Images; SSH8: Ilan Amihai/Alamy Stock Photo; SSH9: Richard Cummins/Lonely Planet Images/Getty Images; SSH10T: Leonardo da Vinci/Getty Images; SSH10C: Pearson Education, Inc.; SSH10B: Evemilla/E+/Getty Images; SSH11BL: Education Images/Universal Images Group Editorial/Getty Images; SSH11BR: New York Daily News/Getty Images; SSH11TL: Library of Congress Prints and Photographs Division[LC-USZ62-39163]; SSH11TR: DNY59/E+/Getty Images; SKHB: Maksym Yemelyanov/Alamy Stock Photo;

Chapter 01

001: Wavebreak Media ltd Ph44/Alamy Stock Photo; 004: Fstop123/E+/Getty Images; 005: Stacy Walsh Rosenstock/Alamy Stock Photo; 006: Ariel Skelley/Blend Images/Getty Images; 008: Everett Historical/Shutterstock; 009: Everett Historical/Shutterstock; 010: ZUMA Press Inc/Alamy Stock Photo; 011L: Auscape/Universal Images Group/Getty Images; 011R: IS305/Image Source/Alamy Stock Photo; 012: Micromonkey/Fotolia; 016: Stockbroker/Mbi/Alamy Stock Photo; 019: Erik Isakson/Tetra Images/Alamy Stock Photo; 020: Stockbroker/MBI/Alamy Stock Photo; 021L: Kablonk/Purestock/Alamy Stock Photo; 021R: Marc Dufresne/E+/Getty Images; 022: Pearson Education, Inc.; 026: Dennis MacDonald/age fotostock/Alamy Stock Photo; 030: Bikeriderlondon/Shutterstock; 032: Bettmann/Getty Images; 032bkgd: Fckncg/123RF; 034B: Zack Frank/Fotolia; 034T: Anthony Berger/Library of Congress Prints and Photographs Division[LC-DIG-ppmsca-19305]; 035: Monkey Business Images/Shutterstock;

Chapter 02

038-039: Inti St Clair/Blend Images/Alamy Stock Photo; 044L: Pirita/Shutterstock; 044M: Petr Bonek/Shutterstock; 044R: Sergey Ryzhov/Fotolia; 047B: Sandstone/Alamy Stock Photo; 047T: Peter Titmuss/Alamy Stock Photo; 050: Kenneth Graff/Hemera/Getty Images; 054: RosalreneBetancourt 5/Alamy Stock Photo; 056: Iofoto/Fotolia; 059: Hurst Photo/Shutterstock; 062: Gilbert Rondilla Photography/Moment/Getty Images; 063: Glowimages/Getty Images; 064: Judy Bellah/Alamy Stock Photo; 066: Yato Rurouni/Alamy Stock Photo; 068B: Granger, NYC; 068T: Larry Geddis/Alamy Stock Photo;

Chapter 03

072-073: Thinkstock Images/Stockbyte/Getty Images; 076: KidStock/Blend Images/Getty Images; 077: Daniel Boczarski/Redferns/Getty Images; 078: Suresh50/Fotolia; 079: E+/FatCamera/Getty Images; 082: Allan Baxter/Photodisc/Getty Images; 083: Palette7/Shutterstock; 085L: Tab1962/iStock/Getty Images; 085R: Jacob Termansen and Pia Marie Molbech/Dorling Kindersley/Getty Images; 087: Susan Law Shin/Shutterstock; 088: Michael Ventura/Alamy Stock Photo; 092: Elyse Lewin/Photographer's Choice/Getty Images; 093: Sheridan Libraries/Levy/Gado/Archive Photos/Getty Images; 094: Soule Photograph Company/Library of Congress[LC-USZ62-104576]; 097B: Glasshouse Images/JT Vintage/Alamy Stock Photo; 097T: IanDagnall Computing/Alamy Stock Photo; 098L: Michael Ochs Archives/Getty Images; 098R: Arthur Schatz/The Life Picture Collection/Getty Images; 100: White House Photo/Alamy Stock Photo; 101: Gabrielle Lurie/AFP/Getty Images; 102: Keneva Photography/Shutterstock; 104: Nicholas Kamm/AFP/Getty Images; 105: Blend Images - Ariel Skelley/Brand X Pictures/Getty Images; 106B: Randy Duchaine/Alamy Stock Photo; 106T: Everett Historical/Shutterstock; 107CL: Gabrielle Lurie/AFP/Getty Images; 107CR: Mtsaride/Fotolia; 107L: Dade72/Fotolia; 107R: Dfikar/Fotolia; 108BL: IanDagnall Computing/Alamy Stock Photo; 108BR: Michael Ochs

Archives/Getty Images; 108TC: Andersen Ross/Palladium/ AGE Fotostock; 108TL: Bochkarev Photography/ Shutterstock; 108TR: Thomas Barwick/Digital Vision/ Getty Images;

Chapter 04

110-111: Curt Teich Postcard Archives/Glow Images; 114L: Korvit/Shutterstock; 114R: Korvit/Fotolia; 115L: Korvit/Shutterstock; 115R: Korvit/Shutterstock; 120: Carl Iwasaki/The LIFE Images Collection/Getty Images; 121L: Kali9/E+/Getty Images; 121R: Pacific Press/Alamy Stock Photo; 122L: American Stock Archive/Archive Photos/Getty Images; 122R: Raga Jose Fuste/Prisma Bildagentur AG/Alamy Stock Photo; 124L: Granger, NYC; 124R: Uwe Umstntter/Westend61 GmbH/Alamy Stock Photo; 125L: Lambert/Archive Photos/Getty Images; 125R: Fotoinfot/Shutterstock; 126B: South America/ Alamy Stock Photo; 126TL: Bassano Ltd/George Eastman House/Premium Archive/Getty Images; 126TR: Iofoto/ Shutterstock; 127L: Fstop123/E+/Getty Images; 127R: Ton Koene/Alamy Stock Photo; 128B: Visual China Group/ Getty Images; 128T: Portland Press Herald/Getty Images; 130L: Arnold Newman/Getty Images; 130R: Enno Kapitza/ Look Die Bildagentur Der Fotografen GmbH/Alamy Stock Photo; 131L: John Murray/Hulton Archive/Getty Images; 131R: Tom Stewart/Corbis/Getty Images; 132: Maksym Yemelyanov/123RF; 133: Alexey Pushkin/Shutterstock; 134B: Joshua Davenport/Alamy Stock Photo; 134T: Library of Congress/Corbis Historical/Getty Images; 136: LorenEvans/iStock/Getty Images; 137: Bettmann/Getty Images; 138B: AP Images; 138T: Bettmann/Getty Images; 140BL: Mondadori Portfolio/Getty Images; 140BR: Gavin Hellier/Alamy Stock Photo; 140TL: Alpha Historica/Alamy Stock Photo; 140TM: Performance Image/Alamy Stock Photo; 140TR: Gordon Zammit/Alamy Stock Photo;

Chapter 05

142-143: Tetra Images/Momentimages/Brand X Pictures/Getty Images; 146: FatCamera/E+/Getty Images; 147L: Roberto Lacaze/Alamy Stock Photo; 147R: Glowimages/Getty Images; 148: Jovannig/123RF; 149: Cathy Yeulet/123RF; 151: MarioPonta/Alamy Stock Photo; 152: Fstop123/E+/Getty Images; 153: Lim Yong Tick/123RF; 154: Heidi Prenzel/Alamy Stock Photo; 156L: Andy Dean/Fotolia; 156R: Lang Choi/123RF; 158: Kali9/E+/Getty Images; 159B: Blend Images/Shutterstock; 159C: Blue Jean Images/ Alamy Stock Photo; 159T: Rohit Seth/Shutterstock; 160L: WavebreakmediaMicro/Fotolia; 160R: Deposit Photos/Glow Images; 163: Marc Romanelli/Blend Images/ Getty Images; 164: Digitalfarmer/Fotolia; 165: Louise Heusinkveld/Alamy Stock Photo; 166: Julian McRoberts/ Danita Delimont/Alamy Stock Photo; 168: The Print Collector/Alamy Stock Photo; 169: North Wind Picture Archives/Alamy Stock Photo; 170: Maria Sakovich/National Archive; 178B: Yves Herman/REUTERS; 178T: Zuma Press, Inc./Alamy Stock Photo; 179C: Vadym Zaitsev/Shutterstock; 179L: Alias Ching/Shutterstock; 179R: Lucia Lambriex/ DigitalVision/Getty Images;

Chapter 06

182-183: Esb Professional/Shutterstock; 188: FatCamera/ iStock/Getty Images; 192: Brand X Pictures/Stockbyte/ Getty Images; 194: Monkey Business Images/Shutterstock; 196: Zero Creatives/Cultura Creative (RF)/Alamy Stock Photo; 197: Hero Images/Getty Images; 198: Dpics/Alamy Stock Photo; 200: Ronnie Kaufman/Larry Hirshowitz/ Blend Images/Alamy Stock Photo; 202: REB Images/Blend Images/Alamy Stock Photo; 204: Espies/Shutterstock; 208: Bettmann/Getty Images; 210: Pixelprof/E+/Getty Images; 212B: Dvoevnore/Fotolia